# Unlocking Your Faith Seeking God's Purpose

A Journey of Faith Overcoming Life's Challenges and Embracing Spiritual Growth

## Gary S. Park

# Contents

| | |
|---|---|
| Copyrights | V |
| 1. Introduction | 1 |
| 2. Understanding Faith | 8 |
| 3. Living for God, Not Yourself | 35 |
| 4. Being a Follower of Jesus | 63 |
| 5. Believing in the Word of God | 83 |
| 6. Prayer Life and Mindset | 97 |
| 7. Community and Fellowship | 116 |
| 8. Reality Check | 142 |
| 9. Finding New Beginnings | 159 |
| 10. Building a Faith That Endures | 171 |
| 11. Prove It | 187 |

| | | |
|---|---|---|
| 12. | Rational Minds | 204 |
| 13. | The 4 D's of Faith | 212 |
| 14. | Final Thoughts | 229 |

Copyright © 2024 by Ridingoncloudz LLC

All rights reserved.

No portion of this book may be reproduced in any form without written permission from the publisher or author except as permitted by U.S. copyright law. This publication is designed to provide accurate and authoritative information in regard to the subject matter covered. It's sold with the understanding that neither the author nor the publisher is engaged in rendering legal, investment, accounting, or other professional services. While the author has used their best efforts in preparing this book, they make no representations of the completeness of the contents of this book. No warranty may be created or extended by sales representatives or written sales materials. The advice and strategies contained herein will benefit your life. Neither the publisher nor the author shall be liable for any loss or damages, including but not limited to special, incidental, consequential, personal, or other damages.

Book and cover by Gary S. Park

Website: www.GarySPark.com

# Introduction

Isn't it time to dive into a soul-stirring exploration to discover what exactly is God's plan for you? In a world marked by ceaseless uncertainty, faith stands as a powerful force, ready to transform lives. The God of Heaven ignites hope and protects us through life's most formidable challenges. Jesus, the divine gift to humanity, bridges the gap between us and God, offering eternal life to all who accept Him as their Savior. Together, let's untwist the enigmas of God's will for your life through these chapters.

After Jesus triumphantly rose from the dead, He appeared to hundreds of people, solidifying His message, and setting everyone on a divine mission. The Apostles, steadfast followers of Jesus, were in a position unlike any other. Their unwavering faith was not a mere belief, but a truth for which they were willing to surrender their lives. Each of the Apostles, uncompromising in their loyalty, was prepared to face martyrdom for their dedication to the cause.

Imagine a time when these men of God faced unimaginable horrors: stabbed, stoned, drowned, crucified—some even upside down—skinned alive, beheaded, hanged by hooks, nails driven through their ankles, sawn in half, boiled, burned, and axed. Their true faith was a beacon, determined in the face of persecution, mockery, and death. If you ever thought your life was difficult, think again.

Our society has grown weak in faith. Many people don't honestly understand what faith is. Phrases like "Yeah, I believe" or "I feel there's a God somewhere out there" have become commonplace. However, when it comes to putting faith into action, the stakes are high—people risk losing family, jobs, and friends. The challenge to live out our faith remains as real and daunting as ever.

Imagine an armed man holding a gun to your head, demanding you deny Jesus or face death. Would you stand firm in your faith, or falter under pressure? You might smack the gun out of their hand, but the point is clear: the importance of your relationship with Jesus, and what He means to you cannot be overstated.

Times may have changed, but are they really different?

There's a divine blueprint that outlines His purpose for each one of us. We should strive to align our lives with our Creator's intentions, finding a path to peace and fulfillment that surpasses worldly understanding. People believe they're being holy by not being involved, but in reality, a person can sin by staying silent. If you see evil and don't protest it, you're cooperating with it. True holiness involves courage and the willingness to confront wrongdoing, even when it's uncomfortable. By speaking up against evil, we align ourselves with God's righteousness and become instruments of His justice in our world.

Some people question whether or not to stop cursing, getting drunk, or engaging in promiscuous behavior. Before addressing these issues, it's important to understand that merely avoiding these actions won't lead to salvation. To those who don't know Christ as their Savior and to Christians who desire to cease adverse earthly behaviors, here's what I would say:

Pursue the heart of God, and study scripture.

Wake up each day and pray, God, I want your heart.

Practice gratitude and kindness.

Live with integrity and purpose.

Be available to listen.

The Bible says that if you delight yourself in the Lord, He will give you the desires of your heart. This means God will instill His desires into your heart, and you'll want what He wants. You will see as He sees and respond as He responds. If you sincerely seek God's heart and ask Him to fill you with His desires, passions, and vision, you will naturally stop doing what displeases Him and start doing what delights Him. These earthly behaviors will no longer appeal to you, and you'll realize you don't need them anymore.

True faith goes beyond mere words; it requires action and commitment. It involves aligning your life with God's intentions and allowing His desires to influence your life. When you truly seek God's heart, your life will be transformed, and you'll find yourself naturally moving away from behaviors that are not in line with His desires. This is the essence of living a life of faith—one that is deeply connected to God and guided by His divine plan.

As we tackle this journey, we'll discover that we're not alone. We are companions on a life-changing quest.

Faith is more than a mere concept; it's a transformative force that connects us to God. According to Hebrews 11:6, "And without faith, it is impossible to please God, because anyone who comes to Him must believe that He exists and that He rewards those who earnestly seek him." This scripture verse underscores the importance of faith and our walk with God. It's through faith that we can understand and embrace His plan for us.

Jesus is often called the cornerstone, the most critical stone laid in any building's foundation. Much like the statement, "Jesus is my rock; everything else is sinking sand." If there was ever a basis for your life, it needs to be something solid, trustworthy, essential, and fundamental to your success. This metaphor highlights the importance of building our lives on the solid foundation of Jesus and His teachings.

Creating our lives and marriages on a solid foundation isn't limited to religious beliefs; it extends to personal values and relationships. When our souls are rooted in confidence, they become unshakeable, guiding us through life's challenges and helping us maintain integrity and purpose in all we do. Faith isn't just a passive belief; it's active and dynamic.

In Matthew 21:22, we are assured that with faith, "you will receive whatever you ask for in prayer." This scripture unveils the power of faith in our prayer life, authorizing us to approach God with boldness and confidence, assured that

He is faithful to His promises. Needless to say, there's a huge difference between your wants and needs. Just because you wish to win the lottery, or your pride demands something doesn't mean it involves God's plans for you.

Each of us has a unique role and a personal quest, and soon, you'll have clarity. By recognizing our worth and purpose, we can cultivate a sense of confidence that allows us to give and receive love. This journey of self-discovery and empowerment is integral to our spiritual odyssey.

Love is hailed as the greatest virtue, and it's our confidence within ourselves that makes love achievable. Understanding our position develops the self-assurance needed to love others and ourselves. God's love is the foundation, reminding us we are valued and cherished. Faith serves as a bridge connecting us to God's mission. It binds us together, allowing us to participate in His grand design.

As we navigate these detailed chapters, we'll discover our individual purposes and how they're interwoven with God's larger agenda. This interconnectedness highlights the significance of our faithfulness. Trusting in God's infinite wisdom is not a one-time choice but an ongoing commitment to trust God's goodness and guidance. Embrace the guiding light by allowing the Holy Spirit to lead you, and you'll soon face life's uncertainties with confidence.

Living out faith in our daily lives involves practical steps and intentional actions. Whether through prayer, reading scripture, or serving others, we can integrate Jesus' teachings into every aspect of our lives. Personal stories and examples from scripture provide inspiration and guidance on how to do this effectively.

Faith has the power to transform lives. Countless testimonials throughout the Bible attest to its profound impact, illustrating how trusting in God can lead to miraculous changes and newfound hope. These biblical statements serve as reminders of the incredible potential within a life grounded in faith.

Faith is more than a theoretical concept; it illuminates our mission and God's purpose, connecting us in a meaningful relationship. This journey of faith is an expedition of the heart, a call to live our lives in alignment with God's plan. Embrace the transformative power of faith and let it guide you through life's challenges and triumphs.

# Understanding Faith

Faith is fundamental in Christianity. Many people identify as Christians, even though they have a limited understanding. Some people only acknowledge certain parts of God's Word. Others don't feel they need to make any adjustments to their lives just because they said the words "I believe." A Christian is someone who follows Jesus and obeys His teachings. Jesus came to save the world and forgive sins by being the ultimate sacrifice. Those who accept Christ acknowledge He paid the price and was resurrected. But it doesn't stop there.

You're not a Christian if you ignore the scriptures and Jesus' teachings and live your life however you want. Each of us has to ask for forgiveness for our sins and turn away from our old lifestyle to pursue our walk with God. In 1 John 3:10, we are listed either as children of God or children of the devil. One of the most crucial aspects of understanding God's purpose is the concept of surrender. When we have complete trust, we let go of our own wants and preferences and instead opt to become spiritually transformed.

Acknowledge that God's ways surpass our own. Trusting that He wants the best for us, even when we don't fully understand, is a crucial step toward growth and development. Before Jesus' crucifixion, He demonstrated an exceptional act of submission in the Garden of Gethsemane. As He prayed, Jesus asked if the cup of suffering might be taken from Him. Despite the excruciating pain and suffering that awaited, Jesus surrendered His desires to the Father's will. His unwavering trust in God and obedience opened the door to salvation for humanity.

By embracing the idea of surrender, we can better navigate the difficulties and uncertainties in our lives. It requires letting go of our personal agendas and having confidence that God's plans for us are far greater than we could ever imagine. When we place our lives in God's hands, we allow Him to work in and through us, shaping us into the individuals He intends us to be.

Your faith is not a one-time event but a lifelong journey that requires constant care and development. Just as a mustard seed that grows into a large plant, Jesus said that even a small amount of faith can move mountains, and each of us needs to start somewhere. This growth enables us to face life's challenges with steadfast confidence in God's faithfulness. Faith isn't wishful thinking or blind belief; it's grounded in historical and personal examples of God's reliability. Luck shouldn't be our focus; instead, we should believe in receiving help; sometimes, it's by divine intervention. By reflecting on our past experiences and interactions, we gain comfort and trust in His loyalty, empowering us to move forward.

We're corrupt people, and it's a continuous cycle of ugliness unless we allow the Holy Spirit to change us into a new creation. Faith empowers us to honor God, believing even when we cannot see the outcome. As our faith matures, we can better obey God's guidance and fulfill His intentions. The Bible illustrates the significance of faith and its importance. James 2:17 indicates that faith without good deeds is dead. It implies that our faith holds no real value if we merely profess it without putting it into action. Our actions reflect our emotions, showing how genuine and heartfelt our efforts for others truly are. As believers in Christ, Christians should aspire to make themselves accessible.

## Discovering Your Purpose

Ephesians 2:8 tells us that we are saved through faith, not by our own efforts or works, so we cannot boast about it. This verse emphasizes that salvation is a gift from Jesus alone, not something we can earn or deserve through our actions. It reminds us to approach salvation with humility, understanding that it's not our doing but a grace freely given. When it comes to our good deeds, the motivation behind every action matters enormously.

You might not receive the desired blessings from posting online or telling everyone about your kind acts. True acts of kindness should stem from the heart, not from a desire for recognition or praise. When we seek approval from others, we miss the point of genuine service and love.

Galatians 5:6 states, "The only thing that counts is faith expressing itself through love." This scripture highlights that authentic faith naturally results in love, compassion, and empathy toward others.

Our relationship with Jesus should inspire us to love all those around us, demonstrating the essence of God's love through our activities. We are called to be active participants in God's work, embodying His love in tangible ways. Living out our faith involves more than just personal belief; it requires motion and a relationship. We are to be God's hands and feet, which means engaging with the world and showing God's love even to those who don't reflect the same feelings and temperament.

This active faith fosters a deeper relationship with God, moving beyond mere words to impactful living. As we grow in our faithfulness, we find the strength to believe in the unseen and follow God's will more closely. Jesus teaches us to recognize the willingness of the Spirit while also acknowledging the weakness of the flesh. The Bible is rich with verses that underscore the importance of using it in our everyday lives.

A vital aspect of this journey is to stop complaining, as it doesn't solve anything. Instead, we should focus on finding solutions and taking responsibility for our actions. By doing so, we learn and grow, becoming more aligned with God's purpose for us. Blaming others only hinders our growth; taking accountability fosters maturity and spiritual development. Maintaining a calm and humble demeanor is crucial. Bragging should be avoided, as actions speak louder than words and reflect genuine respect and humility.

By letting our actions speak for themselves, we honor God and show genuine respect for others. Humility allows us to remain grounded and focused on what truly matters. Listening while being kind and refraining from judgment is essential, as only God has the authority to judge. Sticking to the truth and avoiding lies ensures that our lives reflect integrity and honesty, aligning us more closely with Jesus' teachings.

## Three Types of Faith

Faith is not just a single concept but has different levels, intensities, and expressions. The Bible identifies three types of faith. They are:

## Little Faith

In the first Gospel of the New Testament, Jesus mentions having little faith twice. In Matthew 6:30, Jesus tells His disciples not to worry about their primary needs, such as food and clothing, because God will provide for them. In Matthew 8:26, Jesus and His disciples were being tossed around in a boat by large waves from a storm. The disciples were afraid, but Jesus said, "Why are you afraid, O you of little faith?" And as Jesus rose, He rebuked the winds of the sea, and everything became calm. Even when we have moments of little faith,

Jesus has the power to control everything in existence. We must not take anything for granted without appreciating the actual power of God. The Bible's examples encourage us to have unwavering faith in Jesus and rely on Him to fulfill our needs and calm the storms in our lives.

**Great Faith**

Great faith denotes a higher degree of faith and assurance in God's strength and constancy. This kind of trust overcomes uncertainty and wholly depends on God's assurances. It means having complete confidence in God and his promises. The following two examples of faith are a willingness to obey God's Word and know His abilities.

There was a Canaanite woman who persisted in seeking treatment for her daughter in Matthew 15:22. This emotional situation unfolded when the woman was crying and saying to Jesus, please have mercy on me. She stated her daughter was oppressed by a demon. Even the disciples begged Jesus to send her away. She knew who Jesus was and knelt down, calling out Lord, help me. Jesus rejoiced in her faith and healed her daughter. Sometimes, merely talking with Jesus about our desires and wishes isn't enough; it's apparent we all need to know our place. If our worship and prayers aren't sufficient, it's evident that humbly kneeling at Jesus' feet exhibits His authority during our desires and needs.

There was a well-respected Roman military officer in charge of 100 soldiers known as a centurion who trusted in Jesus' authority to cure from a distance in Matthew 8:5. The centurion didn't want to see his servant suffering, lying paralyzed on the ground. Although Jesus offered to visit his home, the centurion didn't feel worthy of His presence. The military officer knew that all Jesus had to do was say the word, and healing would happen. Jesus stated that no one in Israel had such faith and that the servant would be healed just like he believed. These are just two examples of people Jesus praised for their tremendous faith. Great faith recognizes God's sovereignty and knows He can exceed all expectations.

## Perfect Faith

An unshakable trust in God that has been tried and tested over time is what we call perfect faith. It's a belief that endures hardships and grows stronger with each challenge. Perfect faith requires us to wholeheartedly embrace God's plan and follow His guidance without any doubts. The Bible offers examples of perfect faith in the form of Abraham's unwavering resolve to offer his son Isaac as a sacrifice, as mentioned in Genesis 22.

Just as Abraham was about to carry out the act, an angel of the Lord halted him, and God provided a ram as a substitute sacrifice. This profound moment not only demonstrated Abraham's deep trust in God's plan but also highlighted God's provision and mercy. Such examples serve as powerful reminders of the strength and importance of faith in our own lives, encouraging us to trust in God's wisdom and guidance.

Another powerful example is Billy Graham's unwavering faith, which shone through his lifelong dedication to spreading the Gospel to billions of people around the globe. What's truly inspiring is that with perfect faith, the negative opinions of others fade into insignificance. You carry a deep, unshakable conviction that you are fulfilling God's work, guided by His divine purpose.

Perfect faith is a dynamic force that propels us into active ministry. When we practice, we experience growth in holiness, a serene mind, and emotional resilience. This steadfast faith equips us to overcome life's tragedies and disappointments. It also empowers us to pursue our journey with excellence, deepening our love for Jesus and growing in our spiritual walk. As our faith matures, we become less captivated by worldly things and find greater joy within Him. This confidence becomes evident when followers of Jesus actively live out their faith, moving their beliefs into action.

## The World's View of God

Understanding how people perceive God is intricate and diverse, filled with numerous viewpoints. While some individuals share Christian beliefs, seeing God as a loving Father who desires a relationship with His creation, others hold different conceptions of the divine. As Christians, it is crucial to be aware of these various viewpoints and discern what Jesus taught from what other spiritual leaders have added or modified. Engaging with these multiple perspectives and comparing them with the teachings of Jesus can deepen our understanding of faith and God's intentions.

Atheism, which asserts that there is no God or divine being, is one widely held belief. Atheists often base their convictions on observed data and prefer to remain in control of their own lives, rejecting the concept of a higher power outright. Respectful conversations about faith and the existence of God with atheists can challenge Christians to articulate their beliefs and offer logical justifications for their faith.

Although some people who claim to be atheists can't argue with historical evidence from biblical accounts of those who lived and walked with Jesus. Other historians and letters stated that Jesus did exist. Notably, Roman historian Tacitus, in his Annals, confirmed the execution of "Christus" under Pontius Pilate. Jewish historian Josephus, in his Antiquities of the Jews, also mentioned Jesus and his crucifixion despite debates over the text's authenticity. Pliny the Younger, in a letter to Emperor Trajan, described early Christians and how they worshiped Christ, and Mara bar Serapion referred to the execution of a "wise king" of the Jews. These support the historical existence of Jesus and his crucifixion under Roman authority.

Many atheists convert as the evidence proves itself, finding compelling reasons to believe in the historical reality of Jesus and his teachings. These historical testimonies, combined with personal experiences and reflections, often lead individuals to re-evaluate their stance on faith and the existence of God.

Christians can firmly establish themselves in the unchanging truth of God's Word, as demonstrated in the Bible through documented history, while engaging with opposing theologies. The Bible is a trustworthy resource that precisely understands God's persona and goals. By reading and reflecting on the scriptures, Christians can deepen their knowledge of God and gain insights into His character and purposes.

## Engaging with Respect, Love, and Empathy

Christians should approach conversations about religion and God's mission with respect, love, and kindness. Building bridges of understanding requires listening to other people's points of view, accepting the truth of their experiences, and showing the love of Christ in all interactions. Remembering faith is not a static idea or a purely intellectual endeavor. Instead, it's a dynamic, evolving relationship with God that needs ongoing care and development. Faith is cultivated and deepened through continued engagement with the Holy Spirit's guidance, as generated by hearing the message.

Christians should embrace the transforming power of faith in their daily lives as they embark on this journey of understanding more about what they accept. Along with believing in God, active faith entails conforming our behavior to His will. It demands submission to God's Word and a readiness to uphold our convictions publicly. We become living illustrations of God's goodness and grace by practicing our faith through compassionate service, forgiving others, and loving them.

We can better understand faith and comprehend God's ultimate plan as each of us navigates the complexities of how the world perceives God. By engaging differing viewpoints, we can build awareness and extend the love of Christ to everyone, ultimately strengthening our faith and relationship with God. Unfortunately, not everyone believes in the existence of God or holds the same views on the topic. Different denominations preach or teach a different Jesus than the Bible dictates, which can be dangerous because people cannot make up their own God.

There is only one God, and He holds people accountable for their actions, especially those who teach incorrectly. Deuteronomy 6:4 says, "Hear, O Israel: The Lord our God, the Lord is one." Additionally, in Isaiah 45:5, it is written, "I am the Lord, and there is no other; apart from me there is no God."

Furthermore, the Bible affirms Jesus' divine authority in Matthew 28:18, "Then Jesus came to them and said, 'All authority in heaven and on earth has been given to me.'" This verse highlights that Jesus was granted all power, underscoring His unique and divine role in everything and to all things that will soon come.

## The Reality of God's Character

The world's influential view of God often differs significantly from actual reality. For instance, some see God as a distant deity who created the universe but is not involved in people's daily lives. As Christians, we should strive to share the Bible's valid message of salvation and the importance of respecting and loving one another. Jesus is the epitome of love, whose sole purpose was to serve humanity as the Savior for those who accept Him. His life, death, and resurrection stand as the ultimate demonstration of God's love toward humanity, and His teachings have continued to inspire countless individuals throughout history. By accepting Jesus as our Savior, we can experience the transformative power of His love and lead a life infused with purpose and meaning.

These varied views of God can be confusing, but Christians can take reassurance in the clear depiction of God in the Bible. The Bible shows that God is a loving Father who longs to have a relationship with His creation. Another critical aspect of God's character is His omnipotence or all-powerfulness. Job 42:2 implies that God can achieve His will and purpose regardless of obstacles or challenges. The Bible also stresses the importance of trusting in God's sovereignty, as He can build or destroy any person or nation who turns their back against Him. Proverbs 3:5-6 instructs us that when we place our faith in God, we can be assured that He works all things together for our good.

Jesus, through His sacrificial death and resurrection, provides us with justification, sanctification, and glorification, saving us comprehensively from the power, penalty, and presence of sin. Justification is the act by which God declares a sinner righteous on the basis of Christ's righteousness.

Romans 5:1 states, "Therefore, since we have been justified through faith, we have peace with God through our Lord Jesus Christ." Through faith in Jesus, we are acquitted of our sins and declared righteous before God, past, present, and future.

Sanctification is the ongoing process by which the Holy Spirit transforms believers to become more like Christ. Hebrews 10:14 explains, "For by one sacrifice He has made perfect forever those who are being made holy." As we follow Jesus and His teachings, the Holy Spirit works within us to cleanse and renew our hearts and minds, freeing us from the power of sin in our daily lives.

Glorification is the future aspect of salvation, where believers will be entirely liberated from the presence of sin in eternity. Romans 8:30 assures us, "And those he predestined, he also called; those he called, he also justified; those he justified, he also glorified." This final aspect of salvation ensures that believers will one day be fully transformed into the image of Christ, living in His presence without the presence of sin.

In addition to freeing us from the penalty of sin, Jesus' justification provides us with the assurance of eternal life. John 3:16 declares, "For God so loved the world that he gave his one and only Son, that whoever believes in him shall not perish but have eternal life." This promise of eternal life is secured through our faith in Jesus and His atoning sacrifice.

Furthermore, 1 John 1:9 assures us, "If we confess our sins, he is faithful and just and will forgive us our sins and purify us from all unrighteousness." This ongoing forgiveness reinforces that Jesus' sacrifice covers all our sins—past, present, and future. By continuously turning to Him and seeking His forgiveness, we maintain our justified status before God.

## Trusting the Unchanging Truth of God's Word

We can rely on the unchanging truth of God's Word. Trust that God is a loving Father, all-powerful, and ruler over all things. When we seek to understand God's purpose and put our faith in Him, we can experience a sense of peace and purpose in our lives. As Christians, it's necessary to have a firm understanding of faith and how it relates to seeking God's purpose.

Our relationship with God is built on confidence, which serves as the key to unlocking His plans and blessings for our lives. It's impossible to delight God without dedication. Our faith enables us to access His power, love, and guidance. It also gives us the strength to persevere through trials and tribulations. Understanding faith means recognizing it's not simply a one-time decision or an emotional experience. Faith is a continual process of trusting God and seeking His will. We must not only believe in God but also obey Him and act on His Word. According to James 1:22, we can experience God's blessings and plans when we actively live out our faith.

## The One Path to Heaven

The idea of one path to Heaven emphasizes the transformative nature of this journey and the acceptance of Jesus Christ as the world's Savior. Placing one's faith in Jesus is more than just an intellectual recognition; it is a decision that profoundly transforms one's life. The decision to walk the path of faith in Jesus Christ begins a process of reflection and spiritual development. Aligning one's thoughts, deeds, and desires with Jesus' teachings is necessary for this transformational process. Giving up old routines and welcoming new ones that reflect the love, compassion, and righteousness displayed by Jesus is a lifelong journey.

During this journey, individuals are called to examine their hearts, face their faults, and ask for forgiveness for their sins. Humility, repentance, and a sincere desire to follow God's will are essential to reaching Heaven. Through the power of God's grace, believers are given the strength to overcome their weaknesses and strive for a life characterized by love, integrity, and service to others.

Understanding that others are on the road to Heaven is crucial. As Christians, we must travel in unity, offering one another support and encouragement. The community of believers provides a safe space for the development of faith, the exchange of knowledge, and the promotion of accountability. Through the communal component of the faith journey, we can support one another and work together to better understand God's intentions.

All creations, whether angels or humans, are created to love and worship God. No one is equal to or on the same level as God, and no one has the ability to become a God, regardless of what any denomination states. Similarly, humanity is advised not to worship people, idols, or even angels. While it is natural for people to be curious about their existence on Earth, many share the goal of increasing their level of awareness through activities such as formal education and interpersonal interactions. The answers we seek are found in the Dead Sea Scrolls and other ancient texts, which provide invaluable insights into our spiritual journey.

## The Supernatural and Faith in God

Belief in the supernatural has been a constant presence throughout human history. Even in the Bible, stories involve ghosts or supernatural beings. For example, the disciples twice mistook Jesus for a ghost. This shows that the concept of a divine or otherworldly presence was well documented. You cannot trust your soul to just anyone. Faith in God, the Son, and the Holy Spirit are the three pillars upon which Christianity is founded, and placing your trust in a higher power is worth it.

Jesus is the mediator, and to converse with the Father, one must first reach Jesus. To approach God and become part of the heavenly kingdom, one must have faith in Jesus Christ and adhere to His teachings. Only then will they be admitted into Heaven. To be rescued from eternal separation, one must acknowledge Jesus Christ as their Savior. James 2:17 makes it clear that for Christians to practice their belief, they must model their behavior after Jesus, who commanded His followers to love one another and serve God.

Living in a diverse community can be challenging for those trying to uphold their spiritual convictions. To fortify their faith and adhere to the teachings of Jesus Christ, Christians can participate in various spiritual approaches, such as praying, reading the Bible, attending church, and being part of a community of believers. To fathom God's plan for our lives, we must trust what He has in store for us. Jesus said the only way to enter Heaven is by placing our faith in Him. As a result, Christians must act with conviction and steadfastness. Praying, reading the Bible, attending church, and being active in their community are all excellent ways for Christians to strengthen their faith and align themselves with God's will.

## The Weight of Our Choices

Many people don't realize the gravity of their choices regarding how they live their lives. Every day, we make decisions that either draw us closer to the Creator of the universe or lead us further away from Him. It's daunting to think that some willingly choose to live for the world, chasing after temporary pleasures and material possessions rather than living for their soul's eternal sake. The consequences of such choices can be dire, leaving individuals empty, lost, and alone in the end. It's essential to remember that every choice we make matters, and we must choose wisely, living our lives as if our souls depended on it.

## The Urgency of Faith

Living for God may not be easy, but it's profoundly worth it. It brings us closer to Him, grants us peace and purpose, and prepares us for eternity. As Christians, we are called to live out our faith boldly, not just privately but in every aspect of our lives. This means that our actions, words, and thoughts should reflect the teachings of Jesus. The world may offer distractions and temptations, but we must remain steadfast, knowing that our ultimate reward lies in Heaven.

We can learn from the examples of those who have gone before us and demonstrated great faith. Abraham's faith, even when asked to sacrifice his son Isaac, and Job's perseverance through unimaginable suffering can inspire us to trust God even in the most challenging circumstances. These stories remind us that faith is not about our abilities or strength but about trusting in God's power and sovereignty.

Ephesians 2:8-9 reminds us that our faith is a gift from God, and we can rest in His grace and provision. We can trust that our faith will guide us as we seek God's purpose. If we entrust our lives to God's promises, we'll see that He is faithful and true. Romans 10:17 assures us that by spending time in the Word, we can strengthen our faith and deepen our understanding of God and what He desires for us.

## The Unchanging Nature of God's Love

God's love for us is unchanging and unfathomable. He knows our weaknesses, our failures, and our deepest fears, yet He loves us unconditionally. This love was most powerfully demonstrated through the life, death, and resurrection of Jesus Christ. Accepting Jesus as our Savior transforms our lives and fills us with a purpose that goes beyond the mundane. His teachings guide us to live in a way that honors God and blesses others.

Psalm 103:13 beautifully illustrates God's fatherly compassion: "As a father has compassion on his children, so the Lord has compassion on those who fear him." This relationship is built on trust and love, inviting us into a deeper, more intimate connection with our Creator.

The world's view of God is diverse, with beliefs ranging from atheism and agnosticism to polytheism and various religious practices. Christians must navigate this complex landscape with grace and understanding, firmly rooted in the unchanging truth of God's Word. Respectful dialogue and genuine empathy can build bridges, allowing us to share the message of Christ's love effectively.

Atheists, who deny the existence of any deity, often rely on observed data, scientific reasoning, or personal experience. Engaging in respectful conversations with atheists can challenge us to articulate our beliefs clearly and thoughtfully, offering logical justifications for our faith.

Agnostics, who believe that God's existence is unknowable, challenge us to acknowledge the mystery of the divine and approach discussions with humility. By understanding these perspectives, Christians can better communicate the depth and richness of their faith.

## Embracing Faith in Daily Life

Embracing faith in our daily lives means living out the principles taught by Jesus. This involves showing love and compassion, serving others selflessly, and maintaining integrity in all we do. Our faith should be evident in our actions, reflecting God's love and grace to those around us.

Active faith transforms not only our lives but also the lives of those we encounter. When we serve others with genuine compassion, forgive those who wrong us, and love unconditionally, we become living examples of God's love. This active demonstration of faith can inspire others to seek God and explore their own spiritual journeys.

The journey of faith is deeply personal, yet it is also enriched by the support and fellowship of a faith community. The church, as the body of Christ, provides a space for believers to gather, share their experiences, and grow together. Within this community, we find encouragement, accountability, and opportunities to serve one another.

The diversity within a church community, with its range of backgrounds, skills, and spiritual gifts, offers a holistic view of faith. By sharing our stories and insights, we can deepen our understanding of God's intentions and strengthen our collective faith.

Having faith doesn't mean we won't face challenges or struggles. In fact, it is often through these difficulties that our faith is strengthened and refined. Hebrews 11:1 tells us that faith is "confidence in what we hope for and assurance about what we do not see." This assurance comes from knowing that God is always at work in our lives, even when we cannot see it. His will above all else. As our faith grows, we can have confidence that God will guide us and direct us toward His purpose for our lives.

Living with an eternal perspective means recognizing that our time on Earth is temporary and our ultimate home is in Heaven. This perspective helps us prioritize our spiritual growth and the impact we have on others. By focusing on our relationship with God and seeking His purpose, we prepare ourselves for the eternal life that awaits us.

Jesus said that the only way to enter Heaven is by placing our faith in Him. This path requires us to live with conviction and steadfastness, continually seeking to align our lives with His teachings. By doing so, we can experience the peace and purpose that comes from knowing we are fulfilling God's will.

## The Transformative Power of Faith

Faith has the power to transform our lives in profound ways. It shapes our character, influences our decisions, and guides our interactions with others. As we grow in faith, we become more attuned to God's presence and more responsive to His guidance.

This transformation is not always immediate, but it is a lifelong journey. By continually seeking God and nurturing our faith through prayer, reading the Bible, and participating in a faith community, we can experience ongoing spiritual growth. This journey leads us to a deeper understanding of who God is and how He works in our lives.

In a world filled with uncertainty and distractions, living faithfully requires intentional commitment. It means making daily choices that reflect our allegiance to Jesus and His teachings. It involves trusting in His promises and relying on His strength, even when we face challenges.

As Christians, we are called to be the light of the world, sharing the love of Christ with those around us. By living out our faith with integrity and compassion, we can make a meaningful impact on our families, communities, and the world. This call to live faithfully is not just a personal journey but a collective mission to spread the Gospel.

It requires us to look beyond our own desires and align ourselves with His divine purpose. By embracing faith, engaging with various mindsets, and relying on the support of our faith community, we can become more educated than ever before. As we navigate the complexities of the world's view of God, we can find reassurance in the Bible's unchanging truth. By trusting in God's love, power, and sovereignty, we can experience peace and purpose, knowing that we are part of His grander plan. Let us continue to seek God's purpose with confidence, trusting in His faithfulness every step of the way.

# Living for God, Not Yourself

Living for God is not an easy path. It often requires us to go against the prevailing standards and norms of the world around us. Society frequently encourages us to chase after wealth, power, and success, often defining our worth by these materialistic measures. The pursuit of these goals can lead to a life focused on temporary satisfaction and self-centered achievements. However, God calls us to a higher purpose, one that transcends worldly values.

In Matthew 6:33, Jesus instructs us to "seek first His kingdom and His righteousness, and all these things will be given to you as well." This verse serves as a reminder that our primary focus should be on cultivating a relationship with God and striving to live according to His principles. When we prioritize His kingdom, we place our trust in knowing that He will meet our needs in His perfect timing.

Relinquishing our old lifestyle to reflect His love, mercy, and grace takes time and effort. It involves acts of kindness, compassion, and humility, even when it's problematic. We are called to love our neighbors as ourselves, to forgive those who wrong us, and to extend grace to others, just as God has extended grace. This counter-cultural way of living stands in stark contrast to the often self-serving attitudes promoted by the world.

Moreover, living for God means finding contentment and joy in the simplicity of a life dedicated to Him. It's about valuing relationships over possessions, integrity over success, and spiritual growth over personal gain. This shift in perspective allows us to experience a deeper sense of peace and fulfillment, rooted in the knowledge that we are living in accordance with what Jesus would want us to do.

We require continuous growth and transformation. As we seek the kingdom and righteousness, we become more attuned to His voice and become more responsive to our calling. This journey is marked by moments of chaos and disappointments but also by profound joy and spiritual maturity. Every step brings us closer to understanding the depths of God's love and the richness of His plans for us.

We cannot ignore the profound groundwork Jesus laid during His three years of ministry. His teachings, miracles, and interactions with people form the cornerstone of our faith and offer invaluable lessons for our daily lives. By studying and applying the principles He shared, we can strive to embody the values He championed and become true reflections of His love and grace.

One of the central themes of Jesus' ministry was love. He spoke about it frequently, emphasizing its importance above all else. In John 13:34-35, Jesus commanded His disciples to "love one another. As I have loved you, so you must love one another. By this, everyone will know that you are my disciples if you love one another." This commandment underscores that love is not just an emotion but a defining characteristic of a follower of Christ. It's through our love for others that we demonstrate our allegiance to Him.

However, expressing this kind of love can be challenging, especially when our hearts are filled with anger or hatred. Jesus taught that true love is unconditional and selfless. It's a love that forgives, shows compassion, and seeks the well-being of others, even those who may have wronged us. In Matthew 5:44, Jesus said, "But I tell you, love your enemies and pray for those who persecute you." This radical love goes against our natural inclinations but is essential for living out the faith He taught.

To truly express the love that Jesus modeled, we must first address the anger or hatred that may reside in our hearts. This requires a process of reflection and spiritual evolution. We need to allow the Holy Spirit to work within us, changing our hearts and minds. This transformation involves forgiving those who have hurt us, letting go of past grievances, and seeking to understand and empathize with others. Only then can we fully embrace and exhibit the love Jesus calls us to share.

## Walking the Walk

Jesus' teachings on love also extend to how we treat those around us, particularly the powerless and vulnerable. Throughout His ministry, Jesus consistently reached out to those who were overlooked or oppressed by society. He healed the sick, fed the hungry, and welcomed the outcasts. By following His example, we are called to show love through acts of kindness and service, advocating for justice, and standing in solidarity with those in need.

Moreover, Jesus didn't hide in fancy buildings covered in gold or wear elaborate clothing. He chose to be present with the poor and the weak, tending to sinners rather than those who were already saved. This humility and accessibility were central to His ministry, demonstrating that God's love is for everyone, regardless of their social status or past mistakes. Jesus' willingness to associate with the marginalized and persecuted underscores the importance of compassion and empathy in our own lives.

Jesus' approach challenges us to step out of our comfort zones and engage with those who are suffering or in need. It calls us to prioritize relationships over material wealth and to value people for who they are, not what they have. By doing so, we can create a more inclusive and loving community that mirrors the kingdom of God.

In practical terms, this means looking for opportunities to serve others, whether through volunteering, providing for those in need, or simply offering a listening ear to someone who is struggling. It means standing up against injustice and advocating for those who cannot advocate for themselves. It also means recognizing the inherent worth and dignity of every person, seeing them as God sees them. Moreover, the love Jesus spoke of is not limited to our personal interactions but also influences our broader worldview and actions.

It compels us to seek peace and reconciliation in our communities and to work toward creating a world that reflects God's kingdom. This involves addressing systemic injustices, promoting equality, and fostering an environment where love and respect for one another are paramount. A key component of living a life devoted to God is abandoning our unholy behaviors.

Recognizing and confessing our sins and seeking God's forgiveness is necessary. It's essential to consciously avoid corruption and follow God's path. One cannot claim to love God while living a life of disobedience. It's common for individuals to find a convenient scapegoat they can hold responsible when they become unmotivated and fail to accomplish their personal mission. Everyone needs to be self-aware when they don't live up to God's standards. Each of us cannot use the excuse, "The devil made me do it."

The Bible lists various types of sins, humanistically ranging from minor to severe, all of which negatively impact our relationship with God. Sins of omission are committed by failing to do what is right, such as neglecting to help those in need, failing to pray, and not sharing God's love with others. Sins of commission are actively doing what is wrong or harmful, such as lying, stealing, and engaging in immoral behaviors. Sins of the flesh are related to physical desires like lust, gluttony, and greed. Sins of the spirit are related to our thoughts and attitudes, such as pride, envy, and anger. To a Holy God, sin is sin.

## The Fallout

It's believed that humanity could have lived forever without suffering or death if Adam and Eve hadn't been tempted by a half-truth. But since they both ate from the Tree of Good and Evil, they were cast out of the Garden of Eden. It's best not to play the blame game because we're human with faults and imperfections. Any creation can always deviate from the path set before them. Therefore, it stands to reason that God knew in advance that His creations possessed the ability to make choices and that they would ultimately end up on the path they followed.

In the Jewish library, Lucifer's name appears as Samael. In the Talmudic literature, which comprises the teachings and traditions of Jewish rabbis, Samael is documented as an archangel. Understanding the interplay between God's sovereignty and Lucifer's existence can be challenging but illuminating when approached with humility and a desire to comprehend the bigger picture. We know that Lucifer was powerful, influential, and created with a purpose. Obviously, he could lead, cause disruption, shape change, enter someone's body, and cause all sorts of disruption on this planet. We know that God's knowledge is boundless; He intimately knows the past, present, and future. Therefore, it's evident that God was fully aware of Lucifer's rebellion before it occurred.

Despite this foreknowledge, God still created this chief angel and everything else, granting free will, and it was good (Genesis 1:31). The fall of Lucifer was not a surprise to God; instead, it was part of His sovereign plan. When Lucifer rebelled, his name was biblically listed as Satan, signifying the word "tempter" in his attempt to rule in heaven and interfere with creation. God's sovereignty extends over Satan's actions, using him to fulfill His divine purposes. God's plan of salvation, established from eternity past, required the existence of evil to showcase the magnitude of His redemptive work through Jesus Christ.

In Christian theology, nine angel levels are divided into three hierarchies. The first hierarchy consists of Seraphim, Cherubim, and Thrones. The second hierarchy consists of Dominions, Virtues, and Powers. The third hierarchy consists of Principalities, Archangels, and Angels. The Seraphim are described as angelic beings with six wings who stand in the presence of God and worship Him. They are considered to be among the highest order of angels and are often depicted as fiery, radiant beings. Some interpretations suggest they are responsible for maintaining order in the universe.

The Cherubim are a high-ranking order of angels who are often depicted as four-winged creatures with multiple faces, such as a human, lion, bull, and eagle. They are believed to serve as guardians of the throne of God and are associated with the protection of sacred spaces. Christianity mentions them, particularly in descriptions of the Ark of the Covenant and the Garden of Eden. In the Book of Ezekiel, chapter 1, verse 10, and chapter 10, verse 14, you can see what the prophet documented about cherubim being a four-faced angel.

Within Ezekiel, chapter 28, verses 2 and 9 states there was a prince of Tyre who was a man but acted like a god. Later, in verses 14 through 16, the prophet Ezekiel addresses the king of Tyre, who was being rebuked for his pride and arrogance. The prophet Ezekiel compares the king to an appointed guardian cherub who was once in the Garden of Eden. Ezekiel recorded at least six visions and dreams.

There's always been confusion about this passage amongst the readers, as Lucifer has never been listed or described as a four-headed, four-wing creation, nor is his name listed in the text. In Genesis chapter 3, verse 24, God drove out Adam and Eve and placed a cherub in the Garden of Eden with a flaming sword that faced each direction to guard the path to the Tree of Life. Satan was never listed or stated to have a flaming sword, as he was initially recorded as a serpent who nudged Eve to become more like God, full of wisdom and knowing good and evil. Within the Book of Revelation, 1/3 of the angels fell from heaven, and any of these angelic entities could have caused different types of commotion. In other areas of the Old Testament, fallen angels had children with human women (that will be covered in another book).

## Job's Test

Satan challenges and tests the steadfast loyalty of anyone, just as he did with Adam and Eve, Abraham, rulers of the world, preachers, teachers, and even Jesus Himself. However, Satan remains inferior to God and is incapable of taking action on mortals without God's permission. Around 500 BC, when the Book of Job was written, chapter 1, verse 6 clearly confirms an interesting passage. The sons of God came to present themselves before the Lord, and Satan was also present. And the Lord knew Satan came back and forth from Heaven and Earth. Nobody told Satan to leave or shooed him away; it's apparent that angels gather for various reasons. God's plan was, in effect, to prompt a negotiation to prove Job's strength and endurance, displaying the historical aftermath for years to come. As readers understand this account and comprehend the importance of keeping a strong faith, God blessed Job abundantly through his trials by Satan.

This narrative from the Book of Job serves as a profound lesson about the nature of faith and divine sovereignty. It illustrates that while Satan may test believers, his power is limited and ultimately subject to God's authority. Job's story shows that even in the midst of severe trials and suffering, steadfast faith can lead to immense blessings and spiritual growth. God's permission for Satan to test Job was not a sign of indifference but rather a part of a larger divine plan to demonstrate Job's unwavering faith and righteousness. Through his ordeal, Job's endurance and eventual restoration serve as a testament to the rewards of maintaining trust in God's wisdom and justice. This story encourages believers to hold firm in their faith, knowing that God is always in control and that their perseverance will be rewarded.

## Jesus' Ministry

In 2 Corinthians 12:7-10, the Apostle Paul speaks about having a thorn in his flesh that was given to him by a messenger of Satan. Three times, Paul pleaded with Jesus to remove it from him. However, Jesus told him that His grace was sufficient and that His power was made perfect in weakness.

Although Jesus came to serve, not to be served, to be the introduction for a heavenly kingdom, not an earthly ruler.

Many local Jewish leaders didn't care for His mission. Jesus was chased, followed, kicked out of the synagogue, and almost stoned for claiming who He was and His purpose for being there. It was apparent that the Jews preferred their own way of life and refused to accept Jesus as their Savior.

Satan was always there, jumping into Judas Iscariot's body a few times to stir up trouble. Jesus even knew the exact moment it would happen at the Last Supper. As a piece of bread was handed to Judas, Satan entered his body to fulfill the prophecy of Jesus' betrayal. Nothing was occurring by coincidence. In Luke chapter 22, Jesus asked his Father if the cup could be taken away. Jesus knew the complete picture, to become the sacrificial lamb for humanity. Through Christ, God intended to allow a way for people to be rescued by each individual's choices to either accept a Savior or live for themselves.

Though we may not fully comprehend why God created Satan and many other angels knowing of their future rebellion. It's unwise to question or challenge God's wisdom. Instead, acknowledging God's sovereignty and omniscience invites us to trust His plan, even when we don't fully understand it. Satan wasn't banished from anything, as some would expect. This high-ranking angel who was capable of leadership to separate good from evil would continue to change the course of history.

In essence, God's infinite wisdom encompasses a grand design that incorporates both the presence of evil and the triumph of His goodness. Through faith and humility, we can appreciate the complexity of God's plan and find solace in His ultimate victory over darkness through Christ.

Sins separate us from God and require repentance to receive forgiveness. We must turn away from sin, follow God's path, and strive to live according to His commandments. Our relationship with God requires a confession and a connection with a desire to live a life pleasing to Him. If we falter, we should seek forgiveness. With faith and a willingness to change, we can overcome sin and live a life that honors God.

Though it may not always be simple, following God is worth it. It brings us peace and purpose and prepares us for eternity. As we seek to understand our faith and God's purpose, let us strive to follow Jesus' examples to become better people. You must continually renew your mind and seek God's will in all areas. Devotion involves giving God your plans, goals, and dreams, allowing Him to put you where He needs you to be. One important realization is that God's plans for us are far greater than we could ever envision for ourselves.

Are you ready to live a life of purpose and fulfillment?

Living for God is all about asking for direction and wisdom through prayer and meditation. By regularly communing with Him, you can recognize and understand the unique plan He has for your life. But that's not all; humility and a servant's heart are also essential qualities. By putting others first and serving those around you, you'll reflect the love and compassion of Christ in a powerful way.

The journey of serving God is not solitary but is enhanced by fellowship with other Christians. Being surrounded by people who share your commitment to living for God can encourage you, hold you accountable, and support you as you go. Living for God is ultimately a continuous surrender, expansion, and transformation process. Aligning your thoughts, deeds, and desires with God's purpose is a daily commitment. You will encounter His faithfulness as you learn who you are in Christ and find fulfillment in your life.

## The Carefree Lifestyle

A self-centered life can harm our spiritual soundness and prevent us from pursuing God's purpose. Being mindful of the negative consequences and seeking a path defined by faith and kindness is of utmost importance. The carefree and self-centered way of life frequently puts the pursuit of worldly pleasures, instant gratification, and personal desires first. It may result in a lack of accountability, disregarding others' needs, and disregarding moral principles. This way of living is often motivated by selfish goals and can eventually lead to loneliness, dissatisfaction, and strained relationships.

Moreover, the music we listen to can significantly influence our spiritual journey. Many songs today are filled with toxic phrases glorifying cheating, profanity, and other behaviors that pull us away from the Lord. Without realizing it, we can become neutralized by what we listen to, accepting these messages without understanding their consequences. This acceptance can erode our moral compass and desensitize us to behaviors and attitudes that are contrary to God's teachings.

The impact of self-centered living and negative influences like harmful music is profound. They can distract us from seeking God's guidance and fulfilling His purpose for our lives. Instead of being driven by faith and compassion, we might find ourselves caught up in a cycle of temporary pleasures and superficial goals. This can lead to spiritual emptiness and a lack of true fulfillment.

To combat these influences, we must be intentional about the choices we make daily. Choosing music that uplifts and aligns with our values, surrounding ourselves with positive influences, and dedicating time to prayer and Scripture can help us stay focused on God's path. By prioritizing our relationship with God and seeking to live a life of service and love, we can find joy and purpose.

Ultimately, living a life centered on God's purpose involves more than just avoiding negative influences. It requires a conscious effort to embrace a lifestyle of faith, kindness, and selflessness. By doing so, we can overcome the temptations of a self-centered life and the negative messages that surround us, finding proper peace and fulfillment in our relationship with the Lord.

Being irresponsible with significant matters, such as maintaining one's financial stability or effectively managing your time, can make life more difficult and place you in a financially precarious position. When we give into the temptation of life's joys, we risk ignoring our spiritual well-being, which damages our connection with God. A careless life also leads to relationship problems, which can be highly detrimental to all parties involved. Bad habits such as neglecting others' needs, being insensitive to their feelings, or excessively focusing on ourselves may lead to disastrous consequences. Therefore, it's crucial to be aware of our actions, examine our intentions and motivations, and stay on the right path.

We're obligated to live differently as Christians. We are urged to live with meaning based on our faith, love, and service to others. The Bible instills in us the value of selflessness and concern for the welfare of those around us. Jesus demonstrated a selfless way of life during His entire earthly ministry. He consistently put the needs of others before His own and modeled this behavior for His followers. In Mark 10:45, Jesus sets an example of service and humility by saying that He did not come to be served, but to serve others and give His life for many. Jesus taught us that true greatness comes from serving others while putting their needs above our own.

## The Trinity

By sacrificing Himself for the sake of others, Jesus demonstrated the ultimate act of love and service. For His efforts, Jesus is named the Good Shepherd as He leads the flock, and the Lamb of God for being that sacrifice for mankind forevermore. Aligning our priorities entails turning to Him for direction and seeking to accomplish His goals rather than our self-centered objectives. True fulfillment and purpose come from growing closer to Him and gaining a deeper understanding of His Word. Like Jesus told Philip in John 14:9, "Whoever has seen me has seen the Father."

The proof of the Trinity—the three in one—comes from Jesus. The concept of the Father, Son, and Holy Spirit as one entity is rooted in His teachings. In John 14:16-17, Jesus speaks of the Holy Spirit, saying, "And I will ask the Father, and he will give you another advocate to help you and be with you forever even the Spirit of truth." When the day came for Jesus to leave this world, the Holy Spirit was left among us to guide, help, and direct our paths.

The Trinity is a profound, incredible truth; it's foundational to the Christian faith. It reveals God's multifaceted nature and His intimate involvement in our lives. The Father, Son, and Holy Spirit work in unity to accomplish God's will and to bring us into a closer relationship with Him. The Holy Spirit, in particular, is our constant companion, providing comfort, wisdom, and strength as we navigate the challenges of life.

Jesus' life and sacrifice illustrate the depth of God's love for humanity. By following His examples and seeking the guidance of the Holy Spirit, we can align our lives with God's will. This means prioritizing spiritual growth, service to others, and a deep, personal relationship with God. True peace and purpose are found not in pursuing our desires but in fulfilling the divine plan set before us.

The Holy Spirit's presence among us is a testament to God's enduring love and care. Even though Jesus ascended to heaven, He did not leave us alone. The Holy Spirit continues to work within and through us, helping us to understand and apply God's Word and to live out our faith in meaningful ways. This ongoing relationship with the Holy Spirit is a source of strength and encouragement, enabling us to persevere and grow in our faith.

## Searching Within

A selfish life frequently results in a lack of gratitude and contentment. When we constantly pursue materialistic goals and concentrate on our pleasure, we get caught up in dissatisfaction and perpetually crave for more. The Apostle Paul emphasizes the value of being thankful and content with God's provision. The Bible verse in First Thessalonians 5:18 encourages us to express gratitude in all situations, as this is what God desires for us through Jesus Christ. It reminds us to appreciate the good things in life and maintain a positive outlook, even during hairpulling moments. Our attention is shifted from selfish desires to acknowledging God's loyalty when we practice gratitude and count our blessings. By adopting a new way of thinking, we can achieve happiness and contentment that's independent of our environment or material belongings.

Finding opportunities to help and bless others is an active part of living a life with purpose. It entails paying attention to the needs of those around us and actively practicing kindness, compassion, and love. By devoting our time, abilities, and resources to improving the lives of others, we emulate Christ's selflessness and carry out our mission as representatives of His love in the world. When we make ourselves available to others, we open ourselves up to opportunities for growth, learning, and self-discovery.

By extending a helping hand to those in need, we make a positive impact and invite blessings into our lives. As we give our efforts, we attract positive energy and goodwill, and as a result, God blesses our lives in ways we may not expect. By being selfless and generous, we can attain genuine satisfaction and fulfillment. Pursuing meaningful relationships and developing healthy bonds are additional requirements for a purposeful life. It entails appreciating and committing to family, friends, and community ties. By placing a high value on connections, we create a network of allies who lift and support us on the journey of faith.

The Bible makes it abundantly clear that engaging in immoral behavior ultimately results in one's demise. Isaiah 43:11 states, "I am the Lord; besides me, there is no savior."

This verse is a reminder that individuals who opt for a life of ignorance will face the consequences of their choices.

Living irresponsibly and arrogantly goes against God's principles. This lifestyle inevitably leads to a decline in happiness and peace of mind.

King Solomon was attributed to the Book of Proverbs. He asked God for wisdom, and God granted his request. He became known as the wisest man who ever lived, and his ingenious statements and teachings were passed on after 2900 years. His writings contain practical advice and instructions on various aspects of life, including wisdom, morality, relationships, and work. Proverbs 19:15-16 points out the importance of having a purpose in life. It says laziness brings on deep sleep, and the shiftless go hungry. Whoever keeps commandments keeps their life, but whoever shows contempt for their ways will die. The verses suggest that laziness and lack of purpose can lead to a life of unfulfillment and even death.

On the other hand, those who keep God's commandments and live purposeful lives will have a meaningful existence. These verses emphasize the importance of having a clear direction while striving to live a life that pleases God. And just like many others who follow the path of righteousness, it's better to receive blessings from your Heavenly Father versus turning your back upon Him. We are indeed fearfully and wonderfully made.

However, the Bible also calls us to enjoy life and be present in every moment. In Ecclesiastes 9:7-9, King Solomon advises us to enjoy life and all the good things that come with it. He encourages us to eat our food and drink our wine with joy, as God has already approved of what we do. Solomon also emphasizes the importance of enjoying life with our loved ones, especially our spouses.

Solomon reminds us that our time on earth is brief, and we should make the most of it by enjoying the good things given to us, just like one of Jesus' first adult-documented miracles, turning 150 gallons of water into wine at a wedding. His mother, Mary, asked Jesus to perform a miracle, almost implying she had seen Jesus complete this task before, knowing He could do it again. As the wedding staff watched everything unfold, everyone else continued to celebrate; even the host knew the wine was of better quality.

We are all responsible for our actions and should strive to lead a life that reflects positively on ourselves and those around us. Here are some of the principles we can adhere to avoid a carefree lifestyle:

Trusting God with all our heart, soul, mind, and strength emphasizes the importance of wholeheartedly relying on God in every aspect of our lives.

Spend your time wisely. We should use our time to focus on the things that bring us closer to Christ.

Live modestly. We should strive to live a life of moderation and not be consumed by the material things of this world.

Don't be lazy. Laziness can lead to a carefree attitude and prevent us from fulfilling our responsibilities. We should strive to work diligently and faithfully in all that we do.

When it hurts, God is trying to teach you something; nobody ever said life would be easy.

Many individuals ruin something good by believing they're seeking something better, only to end up worse than before. The grass isn't always greener on the other side.

Ask God for guidance if you feel you're on the wrong path, and the Holy Spirit will direct you.

Trust in the Lord, and don't focus on your own understanding.

If you feel like giving up, pray for endurance.

Do not let money, titles, appearances, social media, or achievements impress you. Instead, focus on integrity, humanity, honesty, and kindness.

These principles can help us live a life of purpose pleasing to God. Living according to these principles means we'll have less to worry about. The carefree and egotistical way of life opposes what the Bible teaches and prevents us from fulfilling God's plan. We can achieve joy and deep connections with God and others by embracing a purpose-driven life motivated by faith, selflessness, gratitude, and service.

## Leaving God in the Building

Attending church has long been regarded as a cornerstone of spiritual practice for many believers. However, the mere act of attending Sunday service without embodying one's faith throughout the week can lead to significant spiritual pitfalls. This phenomenon, known as "leaving God in the building," underscores the challenges of true faith and failing to integrate it into daily life. In these situations, we run into the problems that arise when individuals attend church and engage in the service but neglect to carry their faith beyond the church walls.

The term "Sunday Christian" describes individuals prioritizing church attendance on Sundays while compartmentalizing their faith for the rest of their lives. This syndrome often manifests in the form of attending church services while neglecting deeper spiritual practices such as prayer, Bible study, and service to others. For these individuals, church becomes a ritualistic obligation rather than a transformative spiritual experience.

One common manifestation of the Sunday Christian syndrome is skipping Sunday school or other educational components of church services. Sunday school provides an opportunity for believers to deepen their understanding of Scripture, engage in meaningful discussions, and cultivate community with fellow believers. However, those who habitually skip Sunday school miss out on crucial opportunities for spiritual growth and fellowship. As a result, their understanding of faith remains shallow, and they struggle to apply biblical principles to their daily lives.

Many individuals who attend church sporadically engage in the practice of "playing the part" of a believer during Sunday services. They may participate in worship, recite prayers, and engage in outward displays of faith, yet fail to embody the core values of Christianity in their everyday interactions. The root of the problem lies in the failure to integrate their faith into motion. By restricting God to a designated time and space, faith is confined to picking and choosing and holds little relevance outside the property. This limited view of spirituality inhibits personal growth, stifles intimacy with God, and undermines the transformative power.

True spiritual maturity entails recognizing that God is not confined to a specific time or place but permeates every aspect of existence. Embracing God seven days a week requires a holistic approach to spirituality that integrates faith into every facet of life. It involves cultivating a vibrant prayer life, studying Scripture regularly, and actively seeking opportunities to serve others in love and humility. This discrepancy between outward appearances and internal convictions breeds hypocrisy and undermines the authenticity of your faith.

We can't rely on others to lead us; we must take the initiative, show our faith, and demonstrate how to make a meaningful impact on our lives and those around us. People should be heading to Jesus, not dragging their feet. Since everyone's relationship with God is unique, these are some basic actions anyone can use to keep God in their life.

Pray regularly. Praying allows us to connect with God and draw close to Him. You only get better by practicing.

Read and contemplate God's Word. Reading the Bible is a great way to understand the teachings of Jesus and how to live as a follower of Christ.

Show compassion to others. Demonstrate God's love by treating others with kindness.

Serve in your church. Look for ways to serve and volunteer in your local community.

Live out what you believe. Let your actions reflect your faith, and don't stop sharing your beliefs with others.

These are just a few suggestions to get you started. It's about making a conscious decision to incorporate God into your day-to-day routine. One of the advantages of keeping God close is the sense of tranquility and satisfaction it brings. It can bring happiness to a person's life, especially when you have someone special to rely on during difficult times. Discussing spiritual topics with those who are knowledgeable and experienced can also be beneficial. It can increase confidence and can bring a great sense of comfort. It can help bring others closer to God, providing assurance and strength. We are all called to share the Gospel and teach others about Jesus' teachings.

# Being a Follower of Jesus

Our journey begins with a spiritual rebirth, acknowledging Jesus as our Lord and Savior. Jesus, the carpenter, creates wonderful people by tailoring each of us just right. Faith isn't just a concept; it's a dynamic lifestyle centered on Jesus Christ. As Christians, our lives revolve around His teachings, values, and principles, guiding our every decision and action. Surrendering to Christ signifies indulging ourselves entirely in His divine will, allowing His love to shape our character and purpose. Following Jesus entails actively emulating His examples and selflessly serving others.

Just like taking the time to read Scripture to focus on healthy biblical habits, we must be well-rounded to take care of ourselves. This includes getting enough exercise, ensuring we get sufficient sleep, continually learning new things, and avoiding spending too much time indoors. We need to regularly reevaluate our lives from the big picture while getting out there to see nature.

To deepen our faith, we must engage in practices like reading the Bible, praying, and seeking guidance from the Holy Spirit. These disciplines empower us to understand the essence of our faith more profoundly and share it effectively with those around us.

Community is a crucial aspect; the journey of faith is not meant to be taken alone. God intends for His Church to be a place where we can find accountability, support, and encouragement. We can learn from one another, share our experiences, and encourage one another to love and do good deeds by spending time in fellowship with other believers. Jesus calls us to live obediently and be compliant as His followers. Obedience is a response to love, devotion, and being able to follow directives and instructions out of respect.

Compliance is living a moral or ethical life while understanding life has consequences for our actions because God seeks justice and our heart's integrity. Our desire to honor and please God in every facet of our lives stems from our enduring love and acceptance. Jesus requires us to submit to His divine authority. It entails recognizing that He is the Lord and Master of our lives while putting our faith in His decisions and principles rather than our own. When we surrender, we rely entirely on Him and relinquish our independence.

# The Number 12

Being a follower of Jesus brings into focus the significant and recurring use of the number twelve in the Bible, illustrating divine order and completeness. The twelve tribes of Israel, formed by the descendants of Jacob's twelve sons, symbolize the foundation of God's chosen people (Genesis 49:28). Likewise, Jesus chose twelve Apostles to be His closest followers and messengers, reinforcing this foundational theme (Matthew 10:1-4).

The high priest's breastplate featured twelve stones, each representing one of the twelve tribes, signifying the unity and intercession for all of Israel (Exodus 28:21). In a mission of exploration, Moses sent twelve spies to Canaan, one from each tribe, to scout the Promised Land, underscoring the comprehensive inclusion of all tribes in God's plan (Numbers 13:1-16).

The Book of Revelation highlights the New Jerusalem, adorned with twelve gates, each guarded by an angel, twelve foundations bearing the names of the twelve Apostles, and the city's divine design, reflecting the significance of the number twelve in God's ultimate plan (Revelation 21:12-14). In the Gospels, after Jesus fed five thousand people, the collection of twelve baskets of leftover fragments symbolizes abundance and the sufficiency of God's provision (Matthew 14:20).

When the Israelites camped at Elim, they found twelve wells of water, providing for their needs and signifying God's provision in their journey (Exodus 15:27). Jesus' miraculous healing of a woman who had suffered for twelve years and His raising of a twelve-year-old girl from the dead, demonstrate His compassion and divine power (Mark 5:25-34, Mark 5:42).

At the age of twelve, Jesus was found in the Temple, engaging with teachers and showcasing His wisdom and understanding (Luke 2:42-47). The Ark of the Covenant also has a significant twelve, with twelve stones taken from the Jordan River to serve as a memorial for the Israelites' crossing, representing the unity and collective memory of all twelve tribes (Joshua 4:9).

Additionally, King Solomon appointed twelve governors over Israel, ensuring the kingdom's governance (1 Kings 4:7). Finally, Revelation presents a vision of a woman crowned with twelve stars, symbolizing a divine and complete order (Revelation 12:1).

Through these numerous instances, the number twelve emphasizes the harmony, completeness, and divine governance in God's plan. By recognizing these patterns, we can better understand the interconnectedness and purpose of God's design, reinforcing our faith and trust in His divine order.

## Power of the Holy Spirit

The Apostle Paul stated that he had been crucified with Christ and that he no longer lives, but Christ lives in him. The Holy Spirit can work through us and use our lives to fulfill a larger purpose. After Jesus' resurrection and ascension to Heaven, He fulfilled a promise by sending the Holy Spirit to be with believers. The presence of the Holy Spirit is evident throughout the Bible, from Genesis chapter 1, through the teachings of Jesus and the early church. This constant companionship is a reminder that we are never alone; we always have a Helper to guide, comfort, and empower us to accomplish anything.

The Holy Spirit's presence is not confined to a specific place or time but extends to every aspect of our lives, offering wisdom and strength in times of need. Living from an eternal perspective is foundational to following Jesus faithfully. Despite the trials and joys of earthly life, our faithful citizenship lies in Heaven. The Apostle Paul emphasized this truth, urging believers to fix their eyes on the eternal glory. Such a perspective instills hope and encourages us to live in anticipation of God's fulfilling promises. When we view life from an eternal standpoint, we recognize that temporary struggles are overshadowed by the infinite joy that awaits us in the life after this.

Jesus emphasized the necessity of laying down our lives and taking up our cross to follow Him. This usually requires surrendering our desires, plans, comfort, security, or reputation. Following Jesus isn't just about accepting His teachings intellectually; it's about embodying them in our daily lives, even when it means going against the grain of societal norms. The majority of the world will be against changing their lifestyles as they prefer their own. Failure to grow roots in your beliefs will subject your soul to a weak body, and you'll wither away.

Though the path of discipleship may be challenging, it leads to genuine joy and peace. Trusting in Jesus enables us to be guided toward His perfect plan. Our faith in Him provides the strength and courage needed to overcome life's trials, knowing that nothing can separate us from His love. Even in the midst of adversity, our faith sustains us, reminding us that God's grace is more than sufficient to see us through every circumstance. We must light our candles and shine or fall into the shadows with the rest of this planet.

As faithful followers of Jesus, our mission is to spread His message of hope to the world. We become His hands and feet, illuminating the darkness with His light and offering healing and comfort to those in need. In our pursuit of understanding, let us always remember that our ultimate purpose is to glorify God and advance His kingdom. With each step we take in obedience, we participate in God's redemptive work.

## Constructing a Life of Faith

Throughout the Bible, God's instructions on building and constructing serve as powerful metaphors for the spiritual growth and development of believers. From the Old Testament's detailed architectural designs to the New Testament's spiritual applications, these passages illustrate how God is always available to guide and shape us into the people He wants us to be.

In the Old Testament, we see God's meticulous attention to detail in His instructions for constructing sacred spaces. In Genesis 6-9, God provides Noah with specific directions to build the Ark, ensuring the survival of humanity and animals during the flood. Similarly, in Exodus 25-30 and 35-40, God gives Moses precise blueprints for the Tabernacle, a portable sanctuary that would serve as His dwelling place among the Israelites. These detailed instructions continue with Solomon's construction of the Temple in 1 Kings 6-7, where the Temple's design reflects the grandeur and holiness of God's presence.

Additionally, the Ark of the Covenant, as described in Exodus 25:10-22 and Deuteronomy 10:1-5, symbolizes God's covenant with His people and serves as a reminder of His promises and guidance. The Altar of Burnt Offering (Exodus 27:1-8) and the Bronze Basin (Exodus 30:17-21) further emphasize the importance of purification and atonement in maintaining a relationship with God.

Moving to the New Testament, the teachings of Jesus and the Apostles provide a spiritual dimension to the concept of building. In Matthew 7:24-27, Jesus illustrates the importance of building one's life on the solid foundation of His teachings, comparing it to a wise man who builds his house on a rock. This metaphor highlights the necessity of grounding our lives in the principles of faith.

In Matthew 16:18, Jesus tells Peter, "And I tell you that you are Peter, and on this rock, I will build my church," indicating the spiritual construction of the church on a firm foundation. One of the most profound declarations of Jesus regarding construction comes in John 2:19, where He says, "Destroy this temple, and I will raise it again in three days."

While those around Him believed He was speaking of the physical Temple in Jerusalem, Jesus was actually referring to His body and His resurrection. This statement foreshadowed His death and resurrection, illustrating that through Him, God was constructing a new covenant and a spiritual temple, not made with hands but with His sacrificial love and divine power.

Paul's letters further expand on this idea. In Ephesians 2:19-22, he describes believers as being built together into a holy temple, with Jesus as the chief cornerstone. This imagery conveys the unity of the Christian community, grounded in Christ's teachings. In 1 Corinthians 3:9-11, Paul emphasizes the importance of building on the foundation of Jesus Christ, cautioning believers to construct their lives with care and integrity.

Peter also contributes to this theme in 1 Peter 2:4-5, where he refers to believers as "living stones" being built into a spiritual house. This passage underscores the dynamic and ongoing process of spiritual growth and formation. Jesus' parable in Luke 14:28-30 about counting the cost before building a tower reminds us to consider the commitment and dedication required to follow Him faithfully.

These biblical passages, both from the Old and New Testaments, collectively demonstrate that God is always available to construct and guide each one of us. Whether through the physical structures of the Old Testament or the spiritual foundations of the New Testament, God's desire to shape and mold His people is evident. By following His instructions and aligning our lives with His will, we become part of a grand design built on the unshakable foundation.

## Incorporating Jesus into Our Lives

As believers, it's upon us to share the transformative message. Witnessing to others the valuable information within God's Word is more important than ever. Whether inviting others to church, sharing personal testimonies, or simply embodying Christ's love in our daily interactions, we are called to be witnesses of His grace, mercy, and redemption. Witnessing takes various forms, from acts of kindness to heartfelt conversations about our faith.

Our actions often speak louder than words, demonstrating the depth of devotion in tangible ways. It's essential to approach witnessing with humility, respecting diverse perspectives while sharing the hope we have in Christ with gentleness and respect. Prayer forms the backbone of our relationships; people shouldn't only pray when times are tough; it should be the focal point of everything. Jesus' commission to make disciples remains as relevant today as ever, urging us to share the Gospel with sincerity and passion. Let us embrace this divine calling with courage and compassion, extending Christ's invitation of salvation to all.

Fostering a spirit of gratitude is vital in weaving Jesus into the fabric of our lives. Gratitude redirects our focus from challenges to blessings, fostering a deeper appreciation for Christ's presence in every circumstance. In Philippians 4:6-7, the Apostle Paul encourages us to bring our concerns to God in prayer, accompanied by thanksgiving, assuring us of divine peace and provision in the midst of life's storms.

Disciplines such as prayer, meditation, Bible study, and fasting deepen our connection with Jesus.

Fasting, for instance, allows us to seek God's guidance and sustenance by skipping a meal while elevating the importance of our prayer. At the same time, meditation cultivates mindfulness of God's presence, inviting the Holy Spirit to illuminate truths and insights that transform our hearts. Corporate worship serves as a sacred space for encountering Jesus and fostering community among believers. We invite Jesus to transform us through worship, renewing our minds in a church setting. In our collective praise, we acknowledge Jesus' sovereignty and express our gratitude for a spirit rejuvenation.

## Embracing Spiritual Growth

Guarding our minds against negative influences is paramount in nurturing our relationship with God. By filtering our media consumption and fostering healthy relationships, we create space for the Spirit to dwell within us and guide our thoughts and actions. Active engagement in the Christian community provides vital support, accountability, and fellowship on our spiritual journey. Together, we learn, serve, and grow, embodying Jesus' commandment to love one another as He has loved us.

Prayer and Bible study are foundational practices that deepen our relationship with God and illuminate His purpose for our lives. Through Scripture, we discern God's will and receive guidance for our daily walk. Serving others in Jesus' name embodies His selfless love and extends His grace to humanity, reflecting His character to the world. By embracing a life of purpose, we discover fulfillment and joy in serving God and others simultaneously. Ultimately, placing Jesus at the center infuses every aspect with meaning and significance as we walk in His light.

There was a time when Jesus told His disciples to let the children come to Him and not to hinder them. Life 2000 years ago was completely different than it is now. Children and women were traded or sold as property, and nothing was equal for mankind. Nobody or any religion should put obstacles in the way of seeking God. Although there were many writers in the Bible, you'll see a vast difference between the documented scriptures of how the people comprehended the circumstances versus how Jesus debunks every one of them. Many churches don't allow women to have leadership roles, but Jesus never talked down to a woman or child.

In Galatians 3:28, there's a verse written by the Apostle Paul, who wrote many of the letters that make up the New Testament. The letter to the Galatians was composed in the mid-first century and was addressed to a group of churches in the region of Galatia, which is now modern-day Turkey; you probably heard of it. In this verse, Paul is making the statement that in Christ, there is no distinction between different groups of people, such as Jews and Gentiles, enslaved people and free people, or men and women. Instead, all are equal in the eyes of God.

Never mix negative words with actions, as you're hindering the Kingdom of God. People forget what a church is in the first place; it's not the building, it's the people. When groups have spiritual retreats, seminars, and classes to better their hearts and souls, they're really impactful. And in reality, churches are everywhere, whether it be someone leading a study through a book or some of the new internet sites that bring people to God. Be involved, attend any of them, or lead your own project; God will not stand for selfish ambitions to halt His progress.

If anyone becomes limited in their capabilities, they won't have the reins on their own life. They'll become undervalued and subjected to those around them, and they will internally question the reality in which they live. In Acts, chapter 16, verses 13-15, the passage describes how Paul and Silas encountered Lydia, a notable woman, by the riverside where women had gathered for prayer. Lydia became one of the early converts to Christianity and significantly extended the faith in the area.

Religious leaders sometimes habitually choose which verses they use to manage social influence. It's not their fault, just like students in college or those who've attended seminary to obtain credentials for education or leadership opportunities. There's a set vision and focus point that derives from any religious denomination or particular convention that makes them all different from one another. People are directed to follow the instructions or to have the same opinion as those before them.

Many ongoing relationship issues are derived from old-fashioned habits that prevent a beautiful unity. Similarly, 17% of the world's population believes that specific religious individuals are closer to God, unaware that each person possesses equal capabilities for communication, prayer, and seeking answers. Another example is that during Jesus' time, only a few people truly comprehended the complexity of Jesus being a Heavenly King versus a potential worldly leader. We read many moments in the Bible when Jesus corrects His men about how they should feel or act. Sometimes, people need to think, what would Jesus do?

## Involving God in Your Family's Life

Faith guides us toward our purpose and provides a compass. It's imperative to involve God not only in our personal lives but also in our family dynamics to deepen our understanding of our shared goals and values. Incorporating God necessitates intentional practices such as prayer, Bible study, and active participation in a church community. We seek divine wisdom, strength, and guidance through these traditions to navigate life's complexities:

Prayer can help deepen the connection between family members and God, as it allows for open communication and sharing of concerns and gratitude.

Reading and studying the Bible together can provide a foundation for understanding God's teachings and how to apply them in daily life.

Serving others as a family can help foster compassion and empathy and provide a sense of purpose that makes everyone feel great.

Encouraging spiritual growth and exploration in children can help them develop a strong sense of morality and values.

Having faith-based conversations and discussions as a family can help build trust, understanding, and a sense of unity in beliefs.

Through prayer, we acknowledge God's sovereignty, express gratitude for His blessings, and align our hearts with His purposes. Cultivating spiritual disciplines within our families fosters unity and resilience in the face of life's challenges. Regular practices such as family devotionals and discussions centered on faith promote mutual understanding and strengthen family bonds. Teaching our children the importance of faith and seeking God's purpose from a young age equips them with tools for resilience and integrity. By prioritizing spiritual growth as a family, we instill values that endure beyond generations.

Inviting God into our lives is a transformative journey. By nurturing a closer relationship with Him through deliberate practices and communal involvement, we discover His complete purpose for us in His overflowing love and grace. We create a firm foundation for a meaningful, joyful, and service-oriented existence through faith, prayer, and regular spiritual activities.

## Being Responsible and Accountable

Responsibility and accountability serve as guiding principles, shaping our connection with God and our interactions with others. These foundational values provide a framework for intentional living and aligning our actions with divine purpose. Biblical advice calls us to be moral custodians of God's gifts, utilizing our talents and resources for the betterment of humanity. Accountability compels us to recognize the implications of our choices and to ensure that our behavior reflects our professed beliefs.

When it comes to accountability, we cannot point fingers or find ways to blame outside factors. We are all sinners and fall short of the glory of God, and therefore, we need to embrace maturity and take responsibility for our actions. By accepting accountability, we demonstrate integrity and deepen our reliance on divine guidance and grace. It requires humility and a willingness to learn from our mistakes, fostering a culture of growth and self-improvement.

In our relationships, accountability cultivates spaces of authenticity and support where individuals are encouraged to uphold shared values and principles. Moreover, responsible living extends beyond personal conduct to encompass our impact on society. Our actions and decisions ripple through our communities, influencing the lives of others and shaping the collective destiny. What we do and what we say is closely watched by those around us.

Let's consider some examples of how we interpret the world around us. For instance, is it appropriate to mock Jesus by associating Him with an Easter bunny or another idol who delivers presents by flying through the sky? It's important to remember that Easter is a celebration of the resurrection, just as Christmas commemorates the birth of Christ. Throughout history, people have often distorted and manipulated information to suit their own desires.

During the holiday season, do we stand up for what's true, or do we simply accept what we want to hear?

Ultimately, it's up to each of us to choose how we live our lives, interpret messages, and especially be transparent with our children.

In my household, I wasn't about to lie to my children about some milk-drinking, cookie-eating guy who broke into everyone's house each year to leave a present. I'd be falling to the sinful world by praying and going to church just to turn around and fib to my own kids. We raised our boys focusing on the birth of Jesus and touched base with a St. Nickolas approach to the best of our ability. We explained that Jesus was the present to the world, and we're thankful for His mission to save humanity. We discussed how St. Nickolas was a real person in Europe and always devoted his time and efforts to caring for children in need.

Each year, we'd collect 2-4 boxes for Operation Shoebox Child, fill them up, and bring them back to church so bibles could be mailed out around the world. In addition, we also picked up a few toys and delivered them to our local fire department for the Marine program called Toys for Tots. Although I'm retired from the Air Force, I've been a big fan of the Marines program since I learned about it in 2001. One thing was certain: Christmas movies might be great, but they are terrible at telling lies, especially if the world is trying to displace the Savior.

We all have our favorite movies, and for legal reasons, I won't list them. However, as you raise yourself and your children, each person needs to be aware of what's happening in the world around us.

Integrating accountability into our daily routines demands deliberate action. We must evaluate our motives, deeds, and areas necessitating our personal development. Whether participating in men's or women's or women's retreats, attending Promise Keepers conventions, or attending church services, these are blessings for the taking. Scripture instructs us to entrust our plans to the Lord, relying on His direction and surrendering to His divine will. Through faith and accountability, we surrender control, allowing God to direct our paths, understanding that He is not replaceable.

# Believing in the Word of God

If you're a believer, you'll often receive encouragement to entrust your faith in God and adhere to Jesus' teachings. The concept of belief prompts questions about its essence. Despite the evidence from ancient scrolls, historical letters, and documents, including the rediscovery of words written in the Dead Sea Scrolls, it still confirms the foundation of theology. At its core, faith embodies the deep commitment to believe in something greater than oneself, anchoring the nature of human existence.

The Bible is recognized as the Word of God and is also understood to be the inspired Word of God as it was written by chosen people throughout time. It serves as the bedrock upon which Christians build their faith. This Holy Book serves as our guide, packed with stories of individuals who were delivered from their sins and transformed into faithful followers of Christianity. These narratives vividly illustrate how God intervenes to change people's hearts and lives. Through diligent study of these stories, we gain deeper insight into God, His attributes, His promises, and His divine purposes.

Reading the Bible alone is insufficient if you want to cultivate a genuine faith. Trusting what we read, and believing that God will keep His Word is paramount. It's vital to pray, ponder, and act in a manner that conforms to the encouragement of the Holy Spirit. Understanding and applying the lessons of the Bible involves not only trust and obedience but also a thoughtful and critical mindset. It's crucial to develop habits that encourage reflection and discernment as we work to grow in our faith. Studying the Bible unfolds like a progression through different levels of understanding and spiritual development.

In Level 1, individuals focus on grasping the fundamentals of Christianity and cultivating their personal beliefs. Moving to Level 2, they engage in thorough Bible study, unraveling the intricate events and teachings within its pages and committing verses to memory. Level 3 marks a more profound exploration, where readers grapple with the complexities of biblical texts, exploring themes such as angels, galaxies, missions, and purpose. Here, the emphasis shifts from personal understanding to potentially sharing and teaching these insights with others, fostering a deeper collective comprehension.

At this deeper level, individuals can delve into additional valuable resources such as the Book of Enoch, unearthed alongside the Dead Sea Scrolls in the mid-20th century. This level encompasses an expanded scope of knowledge, including insights into ancient texts and their implications for contemporary faith. As individuals progress toward deeper spiritual intimacy, their prayer life and personal devotion undergo transformation. This change is marked by a profound shift in proximity to God, where the dynamics of prayer and personal devotion evolve to reflect a closer relationship with the Divine.

Journaling is one approach to developing a reflective faith. Writing down our thoughts, prayers, and comments on the Bible can help us comprehend it more thoroughly and clearly. By journaling, we can track God's faithfulness, record our spiritual development, and learn more about His Word. We can spot trends, monitor personal growth, and understand how God has been active in our lives by going back and reading our journal entries. We can also improve our comprehension by participating in theological research and learning. Exploring ideas, principles, and Bible interpretation techniques allows us to engage with Scripture more deeply. It enables us to critically assess other viewpoints and interpretations, fostering a more well-rounded and sophisticated faith.

## Faithful Stewardship

While numerous Bible versions exist today, it's essential to acknowledge the cautionary tone in passages like Deuteronomy 12:32 and Proverbs 30:6. These verses suggest that altering or softening the words of God might invite divine disapproval. In a world where interpretations vary and translations adapt to modern language and context, there's a risk of straying from the original intent of the scriptures. While the evolution of language and culture necessitates updated translations, the integrity of the message needs to remain paramount. It's a reminder that faithful stewardship of the Word demands reverence and fidelity, guarding against distortion or dilution of its profound truths.

The Bible stands as a foundation of faith for billions around the globe, offering guidance, wisdom, and spiritual nourishment. Yet, grappling with its origins and the intricate processes of compilation can prompt profound questions and uncertainties. Recognizing that humans composed their scrolls and letters and curated their contents raises complexities about authorship, selection, and interpretation. Throughout history, various councils and individuals determined which scrolls and texts were to be included, while others decided on alterations and exclusions over time. This intricate human involvement and decision-making underscores the dynamic nature of biblical preservation.

The Gospel of Mark, for instance, remains a subject of scholarly debate, with some questioning the authorship of its ending. Such discussions highlight the complexities in understanding the Bible's formatting and the multifaceted roles of its contributors. Amidst the chaos and uncertainty surrounding its preservation, one cannot overlook the relentless efforts of countless individuals who labored to safeguard these sacred texts. From covert preservation to the meticulous dispatch of scrolls across generations, the journey of the Bible reflects a remarkable history. While uncertainties persist, faith reminds us that God's hand ensured the availability of the texts we hold today. While acknowledging the complexities and uncertainties surrounding its arrangement, it remains paramount to cherish and engage with the sacred texts we possess, recognizing their intrinsic value in guiding our spiritual journeys.

Creating an attitude of humility and openness to God's direction as we pursue discernment is essential. We approach the Word of God with a teachable heart because our comprehension is limited, and God's wisdom is greater than our own. We ask the Holy Spirit for direction as we seek to understand the Scriptures, uncover hidden meanings, and apply God's Word to our lives. In addition, having deep discussions and getting advice can help us discern God's will. We can gain important insights and viewpoints that guide us through difficult decisions or obstacles by asking for the guidance of experienced believers, mentors, or spiritual leaders. We can gain insight from these exchanges and better understand God's agenda.

Prioritizing regular periods of silence and solitude is essential for nurturing our faith. Carving out time for quiet reflection during a bustling and noisy world allows us to attune our ears to God's whispers and discern His voice. Through prayerful meditation, we deepen our relationship with Him and heighten our spiritual awareness. As our trust in God deepens, we become more proficient at applying His teachings to our everyday experiences. In moments of uncertainty or adversity, we should seek His guidance before making significant decisions and find comfort in knowing He's always there.

## Discovering God's Calling

Having patience in God's timing is essential. Often, we may have our own timelines and expectations, but understanding that God operates on His own schedule requires patience and surrender. It's about relinquishing control and allowing His divine timing to unfold, knowing He has our best interests at heart. In moments of waiting and uncertainty, patience enables us to cultivate resilience and deepen our reliance on God's wisdom.

Moreover, assessing our actions and desires is crucial for spiritual growth and self-awareness. It requires humility to examine our intentions and motivations. This honest assessment enables us to identify areas of weakness, acknowledge our mistakes, and seek forgiveness and redemption. By aligning our actions with our values and convictions, we strive for integrity and authenticity in our relationships with God and others.

Ultimately, patience in God's timing and honesty in self-assessment go hand in hand. As we patiently wait for His plans to unfold, we should continuously self-reflect and examine, ensuring that our actions and desires align with His will. In this way, we cultivate a deeper understanding of ourselves and our relationship with God.

But how can we use faith to discover God's proper calling for our lives?

Integrating prayer into our daily routines and family traditions is vital. We must prioritize God's presence in our households and make Him the focal point of all our endeavors. Reading the Bible together as a family and dedicating regular time for prayer and worship are invaluable practices to achieve this objective. When we align our aspirations with God's will, we open ourselves to His guidance and direction in every aspect. Seeking God's plan allows us to harmonize our ambitions with divine purpose, leading us toward fulfillment and spiritual alignment. This includes consistently speaking the truth and apologizing when we fall short of expectations.

To discover God's purpose, accountability and responsibility play vital roles. Demonstrating responsibility entails acknowledging our accountability for our actions to God and others. Mere belief is insufficient; living out our faith in practical ways is essential. This involves obedience to God's commands, showing love to others, and wholeheartedly serving Him. It's about translating our beliefs into actions that reflect our commitment to God and our fellow human beings.

# The Transformative Power of the Bible

As Christians, the Bible is an essential aspect of our faith. It's not just another book but the writings of everyone passing along history while educating the future on what's to come. The Bible guides us better in understanding His plans and how it all ends. Many men and women authored the 66 books that comprise the Bible over thousands of years. Despite the diversity of authors, the Bible has a singular theme: the salvation of humanity through Jesus Christ. The Bible is a compilation of stories and a message of hope, love, and redemption. For more content, you would need to find a particular Bible containing the Apocrypha.

As we read and meditate on the Word of God, we discover His character. We learn about His love, mercy, grace, and righteousness. We also gain insight into how we can live a fulfilling life that glorifies Him.

Testing and Pressure: Your life and faith will face tests and pressures to reveal your true devotion.

Love and Trust: Evaluate who you love, who you trust, and where you place your trust.

Faith and Obedience: Faith is demonstrated through obedience to God's will.

Salvation and Humility: Salvation comes not from good deeds alone but from humility and a servant's heart.

Focus on the Giver: Rather than fixating on life's gifts, focus on the ultimate Giver, God Himself.

Surrender and Avoiding Idols: Surrender everything you love to God to prevent falling into idolatry.

Fear and Sovereignty: Fear God and acknowledge His control over all things.

Redemption through Jesus: Jesus' sacrifice offers redemption, allowing the unjust to approach God.

Sacrifice and Best Life: True fulfillment comes through sacrifice; your best life requires it.

Total Surrender: God desires your complete love, mind, body, spirit, and strength.

The transformative power of the Bible stands as one of its pivotal attributes. It possesses the capacity to shape our minds and hearts, instilling them with God's truth and renewing our innermost being. Rather than conforming to the patterns of this world, our spirits urge us to undergo a change, discerning the goodness, acceptability, and perfection of God's will. Our perspectives are rejuvenated through personal study, enabling us to grasp His intentions and make choices aligned with His character.

Moreover, the Bible echoes Jesus' assertion that heaven and earth will fade away, but His words will endure. The Bible stands as a beacon of steadfastness against the flow of human ideologies. It offers us stability and direction as a reliable compass in a world of shifting brokenness.

We encounter specific difficulties and conflicts daily in addition to its eternal truths. It communicates our fundamental needs, inspiration, and hope. The Lord is our fortress and shield. We don't need to look for love; it's about loving the person we can become.

## Embracing the Transformative Power

The Bible provides spiritual nourishment. Just as food sustains our bodies, the Word of God sustains our spirits. Jesus says in Matthew 4:4, "Man shall not live by bread alone, but by every word that comes from the mouth of God." Regular engagement with the Scriptures spiritually feeds us and equips us to handle life's situations. The Bible provides the necessary fuel to develop our faith, strengthen our bond with God, and bear spiritual fruit.

Furthermore, reading the Bible in a caring community of believers rather than alone is essential. Acts 17:11 gives the example of the Berean Jews, who regularly checked the Scriptures to determine whether Paul's claims were accurate. They studied and discussed God's Word together, advancing one another's knowledge and faith. Similarly, we should gather with other Christians to exchange ideas, debate the Bible, and encourage one another on our spiritual journeys.

We should approach the Bible with reverence, accepting it as the inspired Word of God and acknowledging its transformational power, timeless truth, and practical applicability to our lives. By diligently learning and applying its lessons, we allow them to mold our character and direct our actions. Doing this will enable us to fully comprehend the Christian faith and draw nearer to God, experiencing His desire for our lives and actively pursuing it.

The consistency and coherence of the Bible, despite being written by several authors over many years, attest to its divine origin. The Holy Spirit used these authors to communicate God's Word to humanity, utilizing their distinctive backgrounds, experiences, and writing styles. The fact that these various works gel together to form a unified whole is evidence of God's omnipotence. When reading the New Testament, people will encounter different statements from different writers about the same encounters. Just as in court, where multiple witnesses provide various views and perspectives, these differences enrich our understanding.

One of the Bible's outstanding qualities is its capacity to meet us where we are in our unique situations. Whatever our difficulties, joys, or questions, there's a passage, story, or psalm that brings us peace, inspiration, or understanding. In our lowest points, the Bible encourages us and guides us toward God's unchanging love. From the Old Testament predictions to their fulfillment in Jesus' life, death, and resurrection in the New Testament, the Bible presents a clear picture of God's divine rescue mission.

The Bible offers insight into God's character, advice for relationships, and wisdom in decision-making. By immersing ourselves in the Scriptures, we acquire a discerning spirit that helps us align our lives with purpose. Even though the Bible is the documented inspired Word of God, it's significant to acknowledge that various factors influence our understanding of its meaning. We interpret the Scripture differently depending on our personal, historical, cultural, and social contexts. Therefore, it's essential to approach the Bible humbly and ask the Holy Spirit for guidance if you feel anything necessary.

We can benefit from the rich heritage of Christian tradition as we strive to understand every page. The theological study, commentaries, and experience of spiritual mentors provide valuable insights and help us navigate complex issues. However, it's crucial to examine these sources cautiously and evaluate them against the Scriptures to ensure they align with

God's Word. As we read and study the Bible, we increasingly recognize its capacity for transformation. Engaging with God's Word consistently leads to transformation and renewal.

Let us approach the Bible with reverence, recognizing its divine origin and the significant influence it can have on our lives. By doing so, we understand that the Bible is more than just a book. It's a sacred path leading to knowledge of the faith and an exploration of God's purposes. And it details what happens when Jesus returns. Faith is a conscious decision to trust God and His promises.

Through Jesus, we are saved, enabling us to live a life of responsibility and accountability for our beliefs. It's not enough to say we believe; instead, we must live it and own up to it. We must obey His commands, love others, and serve Him with all our hearts. Our faith should inspire us to be better people, live with integrity, and positively impact the world. Ultimately, seeking God's purpose is a lifelong journey. It requires humility, perseverance, and a willingness to learn and grow. The fact you woke up this morning is a direct indication that God isn't done with you yet!

# Prayer Life and Mindset

Some people have the mindset, "I just want to be a good person." Many strongly feel that the way to Heaven is by being friendly to all those around us. Those who advocate for this basic belief have it all wrong. It's almost like declaring your work and personality is all you need to hit the finish line. Jesus knew we'd never make it on our own; it's impossible to enter Heaven on mortal values. If anyone wants to follow Jesus, they must deny themselves and follow Him.

Are your actions driven by selfish motives?

Anyone who lives in disobedience while engaging in unrepented sin will not inherit the Kingdom of Heaven. People require a transformed life that seeks to follow Jesus' teachings and live up to God's standards. Jesus wants that deep personal relationship. You don't want to hear the words, "I never knew you, away from me."

Those who pray often love praying for themselves versus praying for others. We love asking God to be with us during our struggles and hardships. All want God to open doors to victories. Each of us needs to have spiritual responsibility for one another. Our prayers need to be for what God wants, as His will be done. If you want the companionship of the Holy Ghost, it must be for the right reasons.

Prayer is a way to communicate with God and a powerful practice that alters our perspectives and impacts how we live. As we gain a deeper grasp of its power, we learn that prayer can profoundly affect us. Aligning your heart and mind with practice is essential. We frequently come to worship with our wants and plans, hoping to convince God to grant our wishes. However, as we grow in faith, we understand everything isn't about our desires and needs.

In the Garden of Gethsemane, Jesus was with His disciples, praying and pleading with His Father for hours to remove the cup of pain from Him. Jesus demonstrated an example of genuine submission. Jesus was willing to go to the cross, but He still asked His Father if there was another way to save humanity. There was tremendous spiritual pressure at this moment, where Jesus began to sweat blood as He understood what would soon happen.

Understandably, some might be confused about why I'm referring to it as a "cup of pain," especially since the word "pain" doesn't appear in the original passage. However, the term "cup" is a metaphor used in Isaiah 51:7. The verse speaks about those who have drunk from the hand of the Lord, the cup of His wrath. This metaphorical language is used to describe the punishment or suffering that people may experience due to their actions. In the same way, the "cup of pain" refers to the emotional or physical anguish that one may endure due to difficult circumstances or personal struggles.

The wrath of God isn't about having a fit or being upset. This is furious, righteous anger that God will eventually pour out on Jesus, who would be crucified on the cross for the sins of everyone, including your sins, with full force. A just God cannot sweep sin under the rug. Jesus knew His time was coming, and although He prayed, God did not change His character. Just as Jesus submitted to God through prayer, we must do the same.

We learn to submit our aspirations while comprehending that many things are outside our control. God can grant you favor or deny your request. Prayer gives us a fresh outlook on our difficulties and trials. We can treat hardships as opportunities for growth and improvement rather than just seeing them as restrictions. Either way, we must be persistent and stay focused versus giving up on our prayers.

We need the determination to develop ourselves and become more complete, realizing there's power in devotion. Through prayer, we create the grit and resiliency to confront hardship with faith and fortitude, confident that God is always listening and available. It aids in understanding and appreciation for the numerous blessings we have. God wants you to be thankful in all situations. When we develop better prayer habits, we can turn our attention away from what we lack and onto what we have.

Prayer is not merely a laundry list of requests to be recited; it's a sacred conversation with the Divine. A moment of communion where we express gratitude, seek guidance and surrender our will to a higher purpose. Possessing the spirit of thankfulness isn't only for the blessings we receive but also for the things we lack, recognizing that godly wisdom surpasses our human understanding. We express gratitude for the blessings we have, such as:

The gift of life and health allows us to experience each day with vigor and vitality.

Loving relationships with family and friends, providing support, companionship, and shared moments of joy.

Opportunities for personal and professional growth, empowering us to realize our potential and contribute meaningfully to the world.

Material comforts and provisions, including food, shelter, and clothing, which sustain and nourish us in our daily lives.

Moments of beauty and inspiration found in nature, art, music, and literature that enrich our souls and uplift our spirits.

We should acknowledge with gratitude the things we don't have. Our lives are handled in ways beyond our comprehension. Some examples include:

Particular material possessions or wealth that may distract us from our spiritual journey or lead us away from God's path.

Although we may not receive prompt solutions to our problems and challenges, we can learn to foster resilience, forbearance, and reliance on God's timing.

Delayed gratification or waiting for success teaches us the value of perseverance, determination, and faith in the face of adversity.

Complete understanding of God's plan for our lives reminds us to walk by faith, not sight, and surrender our desires to His greater insight.

Pain, suffering, or hardship enables us to empathize with others, grow in compassion, and draw closer to God in moments of vulnerability.

Even in the depths of suffering, we find solace in the assurance that God's grace is ever-present, offering comfort, strength, and redemption. As Jesus proclaimed, "My grace is sufficient for you, for my power is made perfect in weakness." In our moments of greatest vulnerability and distress, God's grace becomes a source of hope and resilience, sustaining us through trials. Sometimes, our suffering creates opportunities for spiritual growth for others as it provokes them to pray for us. It's difficult to understand how you could be suffering for the sake of someone else, but when someone near you prays, it will help their relationship, bringing them closer to God.

In times of misery, we are reminded that God's grace is not dependent on our strength or merit but flows freely as a gift of divine mercy. It's a reminder that we're never alone, that God is intimately acquainted with our pain, and that His grace is more than sufficient to sustain us through every trial and tribulation. As we place our trust in God's unwavering and unfailing love, we find the courage to persevere, knowing that His power is made perfect in our weakness.

## Profound Blessings

Throughout every aspect of our lives, whether in abundance or scarcity, prayer invites us to cultivate a heart of gratitude, trusting that God's provision and wisdom are always at work for our ultimate good. As we embrace the spirit of thankfulness, we discover profound blessings hidden in life's challenges and find peace in knowing that we are held in the loving embrace of the Divine. We can conquer fear and anxiety by lifting our worries and problems to God. Do your best not to worry and approach God with humility in every circumstance. Besides, worrying is a sin by itself. By giving our anxieties to God, He can touch our hearts and minds to ease the burden. It serves as a reminder that we have a loving and compassionate Heavenly Father who's there for us at every turn.

Prayer is an exchange with God and a way to transform ourselves as we cultivate a prayerful mindset anchored in faith. Through prayer, we ask God to shape our thoughts and desires accordingly. To experience the full transformative power of prayer, we should approach it with patience, humility, and an open heart to receive God's guidance. By developing a consistent and authentic prayer life, we can create a mindset that reflects our Heavenly Father's love, wisdom, and purposes.

Prayer is a vital link between our mortal existence and the Divine. Through prayer, we connect with God, seek guidance, find solace, and grow in our relationship with Him. Our deep connection with the Almighty transforms our prayer life and our future selves. Discovering the heart of prayer unveils a thrilling journey of connection with God, where our words become powerful agents of change.

In the Heavenly realm, there's an electrifying promise: the righteous prayer of a believer holds remarkable power, echoing the assurance of Jesus Himself. Every moment spent in conversation with God unveils new depths of His love and purpose for your life. It's more than a routine; it's a thrilling expedition of faith and discovery, where every prayerful moment sparks divine revelation and transformation. Be involved in your relationship, and let the adventure of prayer ignite your soul!

## The Crucifixion

On that day at Calvary, two men hung on crosses beside Jesus. One of them, a thief, recognized the truth about the man crucified beside him. In the midst of his agony, he turned to Jesus and said, "Jesus, remember me when you come into your kingdom." With these few words, the thief acknowledged Jesus as Lord, and in response, Jesus offered him a promise of profound hope: "Truly I tell you, today you will be with me in paradise."

This moment is a powerful testament to the boundless grace and mercy of Jesus. The thief, in his final hours, found salvation through faith. This story brings comfort to many, knowing that no matter how late, acceptance of Jesus can lead to eternal life. It's a beacon of hope, reminding us that redemption is always within reach. However, for those of us who are not on our deathbeds, the story does not end here. We have the gift of time – time to live, to love, and to demonstrate the relationship we have with our Savior. Our lives become the canvas on which our faith is painted, a living testament to the relationship we uphold with Jesus.

Every day is an opportunity to prove and display the depth of our relationship. This means more than just confessing with our lips; it means living out our faith through our actions, our choices, and our interactions with others. It's about embodying the teachings of Jesus in our daily lives, showing compassion, kindness, and forgiveness. It's about being His hands and feet in a world that desperately needs His love. The man crucified with Jesus had only moments to demonstrate his faith, but we have a lifetime. Let us not squander this precious time. Let our lives be a testament to the relationship we cherish with our Lord. Let us live in a way that when others see us, they see a glimpse of Jesus.

In every act of kindness, every moment of humility, and every expression of love, we are showing the world the kind of relationship we have. Our faith should not be hidden but displayed boldly and humbly so that others may be inspired to seek the same relationship. In the end, our journey is about more than just reaching the gates of Heaven. It's about living a life that honors God, a life that brings His kingdom closer to earth. It's about being a faithful servant, a loving neighbor, and a beacon of hope.

Jesus warned us of those who claim to be followers but don't live according to His teachings. Only those who do the will of His Father will enter Heaven. It's not your confession that grants entry into Heaven. Once again, it's your obedience to His commands and having a relationship with Him.

## Formalities

Jesus condemns anyone who professes their faith but lives hypocritically. People may have attended many churches and been baptized multiple times, but their hearts weren't devoted to God. Baptism, while a significant and sacred act, doesn't save anyone on its own. It's not the water that holds the power of salvation; instead, it's a symbol of the transformation that takes place within. Baptism represents the washing away of the old self and the commitment to live a new life in Christ. It signifies a profound inner change, a turning away from sin, and a pledge to follow Jesus.

However, in some churches, baptism is used merely as a church membership obligation, a ritualistic formality rather than a genuine expression of faith. When baptism is treated as a mere checkbox for inclusion in a religious community, the actual meaning is lost if not explained. The water alone cannot cleanse the soul if the heart remains untouched by God's grace. True transformation requires more than an outward sign; it demands an inward renewal, a sincere devotion to living according to God's will.

Jesus Himself warned against such superficial displays of faith. He saw through the outward actions and looked directly into the heart. He knew that it was not enough to simply go through the motions. A life of faith is one that is lived out daily in actions, words, and intentions that align with the teachings of Christ. Hypocrisy arises when there's a disconnect between what one professes and how one lives. It's this disconnect that Jesus condemns.

Baptism should be a reflection of a true change, a public declaration of an internal reality. It should mark the beginning of a journey, not a mere formality. It's an invitation to a new way of life, one that is characterized by love, humility, and obedience to God's commands. When approached with the right heart, baptism is a beautiful and powerful testament to one's faith. But when it becomes just another ritual, it loses its significance and becomes a hollow gesture.

Let us remember that God desires our hearts, our genuine repentance, and our earnest pursuit of a relationship with respect. He wants us to live authentically, embodying the values of the Kingdom of Heaven in every aspect of our lives. Baptism is an important step, but it's just that – a step. The journey of faith is continuous and ever-deepening. It requires daily commitment, reflection, and growth. Let our baptisms be accurate reflections of our transformed hearts, dedicated to living out the love and truth of Jesus Christ.

## The Importance of Active Prayer

Active prayer and meditation are crucial in our spiritual path as we seek God's will. In addition to strengthening our relationship with God, we are given more opportunities to show others our love, compassion, and selflessness. Being active and praying for others is a crucial aspect of our faith. Jesus exemplified this by being selfless and always there for others, even when it was difficult for Him.

He wants us to follow in His footsteps by comforting and supporting those around us. If we're too self-centered, we might disregard the needs of others and become inconsiderate. Nonetheless, we can avoid falling into this trap by regularly praying for others and extending our support. We learn to put aside our desires and comfort and prioritize the essentials of those around us. This is an important aspect of being an excellent example for others to follow.

Being a prayer warrior means dedicating time to praying for others; you can make a list. This includes our friends, family, strangers, or those who've hurt you. By lifting up each one in prayer, we can display to the Lord that we care and they're not alone. This can be a powerful way to encourage and support others, especially during the difficult times. Praying for others can also have a positive impact on our own lives. When we take the time to focus on the needs of others, we often find that our own problems and worries begin to fade away. This is because we're no longer consumed by our battles but instead focused on those around us. In turn, this can help reduce our stress and anxiety levels, positively impacting our physical and emotional health.

Being available for others doesn't just mean praying for them. It also means being physically present and offering our support in any way possible. This can include things like offering a listening ear, providing practical help, or simply being a shoulder to cry on. By being there for others, we can help alleviate their burdens and show them they're not alone. Although prayer is powerful, people still enjoy the human experience of seeing friendly people in action.

Our purpose as believers is to radiate love and kindness wherever we go. By setting an example for others to follow, we demonstrate what it truly means to be a follower of Christ. Participating in a prayer group is highly effective for strengthening bonds between believers and expanding the church as a whole. The power of group prayers is extraordinary when we unite in faith.

Approaching God with reverence and humility becomes possible when we acknowledge our dependence on Him and His sovereignty. By surrendering our wants, plans, and agendas, we create space for God to work in our lives and the lives of others in transformative ways. To pray for others effectively, we must let go of our own interests and align ourselves with God's plans, trusting that He knows what is best for everyone involved. Prayer offers us a way to connect with God on a deeper level and also provides an effective means of making requests on behalf of others. Engaging in worship not only involves others but also allows us to grow in our faith and demonstrate love, compassion, and selflessness.

Consistent and earnest prayer for those in our community enables us to align with God's heart and experience the transformational power of interceding on their behalf. It's our responsibility to encourage and support each other in our faith journey while also bearing witness to God's greatness. Surrounding ourselves with positive influencers is crucial to achieving success in life, and the people we choose to spend time with and the activities we engage in play a significant role in shaping our life's satisfaction. By embracing these principles, we can lead a fulfilling and purposeful life while positively living up to Jesus' examples.

# Managing Your Mindset and Avoiding Dark Thoughts

I'll share a true story from my life, so bear with me. I was deployed with the military, serving my country. However, my journey took a drastic turn when I was struck in the head by a bomb tail fin during a mission. The impact left me injured and in need of medical attention. After being glued and stapled and granted a few days off to recover, I returned to duty to complete my tour.

Upon returning to the States, I began noticing changes in my health. Though I didn't show symptoms of PTSD, there were moments when my hearing and vision temporarily went offline. Concerned, I sought advice from Dr. Eddleman, who made a startling discovery: a 2.5-inch tumor behind my left eye, near my ear. Immediate surgery was necessary, and I was referred to Dallas, Texas, where Dr. Samuel Barnett would perform the procedure.

Facing this daunting challenge, I found reassurance in the unwavering support of my church family and the love of my wife, who inscribed scriptures on my arms to give me strength. The surgery was intense, with Dr. Barnett needing to remove the tumor by cutting around my face, severing nerve endings to peel everything off, and using drills and saws. Over 60 staples and titanium plates held me together afterward, and as I looked into the mirror, I could hardly recognize the swollen face that stared back at me.

Throughout the grueling two months of healing, I strove to stay resilient, leaning on my faith and the support of loved ones. Despite moments of doubt and episodes of depression, I trusted in the skills of my medical team and the prayers of those around me. With God's grace and everyone's help, I emerged from this ordeal with a newfound appreciation for life and a deeper sense of resilience. Though not an easy journey, I knew that since I'm still here, God has plans in store for me, just as He does for you.

Most people won't endure the mental anguish of a tumor, but many face similar struggles, often through intrusive thoughts. Managing our thoughts is crucial not only for our well-being but also for our prayer life. Our minds are prone to entertain various emotions, sometimes beyond our control, making it challenging to bond with God and discern His plan for us. Negative thinking, doubt, and fear may tempt us in times of hardship, hindering our spiritual journey.

To counter this, we must train our minds toward self-control and positivity. Cultivating an attitude of gratitude, focusing on the good in our lives, and envisioning success can reshape our thoughts and open us to God's purpose. Avoiding negative influences and surrounding ourselves with supportive communities are essential for mental stability and spiritual growth. Despite the trials we face, we must remember that these challenges are temporary, urging us to spend our time on things that bring joy.

Uncertainty, trouble, and anxiety are standard to human experience, striking unexpectedly. These emotions can lead to confusion and frustration, questioning if our difficulties will ever end. As people of faith, we can triumph over such feelings by fostering a positive mindset and rejecting negativity. Utilizing positive affirmations helps prevent negative thoughts from dominating our minds. By being mindful of our thoughts and actively managing them, we gain control over our reactions and outcomes.

Cultivating a mindset of gratitude is a potent antidote to negativity. Take time daily to reflect on blessings and express appreciation, even in simple things like savoring a favorite food or feeling sunlight on your skin. Emphasizing the positive aspects of life reduces the impact of destructive thoughts on our outlook. Surrounding ourselves with positive influences and being mindful of media consumption further enhances our mental well-being.

Regularly engaging with Scripture and inspirational literature reshapes our thoughts and illuminates our perspective. Prayer remains invaluable for managing our mindset and surrendering anxieties to God, inviting transformative power into our lives. By focusing on what is true, noble, and praiseworthy, we can navigate each day in the light, guided by faith rather than dwelling in darkness.

Let us live each day with purpose and passion, demonstrating our faith through actions and love. Embrace each moment as an opportunity to deepen our relationship with Jesus and share His love with the world. When our time comes, may we stand before our Savior not just with words of faith but with lives that have indeed followed Him.

If anyone would like additional information about this subject, I wrote a book called:

Managing Intrusive Thoughts. The Audible is narrated by Helpful Matthew. All the links are on my website: www.GarySPark.com

# Community and Fellowship

The best aspect of understanding faith is gaining more knowledge and wisdom. As loving people, we should desire to be around others and share our walk and stories. The Bible often speaks of believers as a body, each member having a specific function and purpose. We can encourage one another, learn from one another, and grow together. Becoming a church member can provide a sense of belonging and support, especially during problematic moments.

Hebrews 10:24-25 - "And let us consider how we may spur one another on toward love and good deeds, not giving up meeting together, as some are in the habit of doing, but encouraging one another, and all the more as you see the Day approaching."

I have faced numerous difficult situations and appreciate the support and sense of community that comes with being part of a church family. Attending services and events allows us to connect with others, which can be crucial for our recovery and help us avoid isolation and negative patterns. Although some may find Jesus and the Cross controversial, they serve as a reminder to refrain from sinful ways. In church, many individuals are aware of their shortcomings and have sought guidance and forgiveness from Jesus for their struggles, mistakes, and overall existence.

However, some people refrain from attending church due to the fear of being judged by hypocritical individuals. It's important to remember that everyone is a sinner and falls short of the glory of God. It's like stepping into a gym; some of the people are very fit, and others are jiggling and shaking around. Everyone has a personal goal but will only obtain results if they put their bodies in motion. Attending church is not about being perfect or judging others. Instead, it's about enhancing one's faith and building a relationship with God. By seeking guidance and forgiveness within a church community, individuals can grow spiritually and find support in their journey toward a better life.

Fellowship is also about supporting and helping one another; it could be through prayer, meal sharing, or simply offering a listening ear. Doing so builds deeper relationships and demonstrates God's love for one another. In addition to building relationships with other believers, fellowship with God is essential in understanding our faith further than ever before. This relationship is achieved through prayer, reading Scripture, and worshiping. As our relationship with God deepens, we become more in tune with who He is, what He's done, and what will happen in the future.

See what Jesus says in Luke chapter 10, verse 19. "Behold, I have given you authority to tread on serpents and scorpions and over all the power of the enemy, and nothing shall hurt you." Jesus isn't saying find a snake and step on it. He's stating the kingdom of God is coming, and people need to be faithful to His purpose and plans. If you entrust in Him, the world can't harm you. You will overcome the difficulties of life. The faithful delivery of holy authority is a duty, for those who know His name will be granted His protection and guidance.

Having spiritual mentors who have walked the path of faith before us is valuable. They can offer helpful guidance, wisdom, and support while providing us with a fresh perspective on our challenges. There are different beliefs and religions out there, and we should carefully evaluate what anyone tells us against what the Bible teaches. Jesus never preached a religion. He wanted a relationship with each person. His message was about a personal connection with God, not a set of rules or rituals to follow.

He offered a way for people to discover true life and spiritual freedom. Jesus taught that the most important thing was to love God and love others, and this love would be the foundation for everything else. He invited people to follow Him, not as a religious leader, but as a friend and a guide on their journey of faith. Through His life, death, and resurrection, Jesus made it possible for us to have a personal relationship with God and experience love and grace in a real and tangible way. Some people may hesitate to accept Christ, waiting for the "perfect" moment; Jesus meets us where we are and embraces us no matter what.

## A Personal Message Moment

Our faith is a deeply personal journey; with proper guidance, everyone can understand Jesus's message. Discerning truth can be challenging amidst the voices of diverse people from all walks of life. When I was just 4 years old, my grandmother, Mokie, recounted a moment during a church service. The pastor asked the congregation, "Who's ready to be saved? Come forward." Apparently, I left my seat and started walking down the aisle. Was I old enough to fully grasp what was happening? Probably not. Yet, I'm grateful that even at such a tender age, I was eager to experience some godly momentum. Throughout my years, I've been blessed, sprinkled, and later baptized at the age of 19 after I learned some vital information.

Millions of people believe, because of their congregation of church membership, that sprinkling a child or baptism saves you while preparing you for eternity. The Bible is clear that you should repent of your sins, accept Jesus, and live a life that honors God. Baptism is an inward reality of an outward expression. There is no magical power in the water; people may bless it, pray over it, or even do a cannonball if they wish, but either way, it's just water.

When someone accepts Christ, it's common for each person to undergo believer's baptism. This is because Jesus set the example by requesting John the Baptist to perform His ceremony. Everyone who wants everlasting life needs to be old enough to know what it means to follow Jesus. They need to comprehend what sin is so they can repent and wash away the old version of themselves as they begin their walk with God. Everyone who accepts Christ needs to change their old ways to lead a life pleasant to the Lord's eyes. As a reminder, just because someone says "I believe in God" and was baptized won't represent an entry into Heaven.

## Quick Story

Meagan is a devout Christian who has witnessed many baptisms over the years. Her niece was excited about her decision to get baptized, and Meagan wanted to ensure her niece's faith started on the right foot. She recommended waiting a few weeks to grasp everything a baptism represents. Her niece was grateful for many conversations and decided to take more time to study and reflect on her faith before taking the next step. Many churches take records of how many baptisms they performed to display how effective they are.

Her niece was baptized the following month, and it was a beautiful and meaningful ceremony. Meagan was proud of her niece for taking the time to understand what her commitment to Jesus entails. Meagan's wise decision to prioritize her niece's spiritual growth instead of rushing into the ceremony was a testament to her devotion to helping others embrace their faith with more understanding. It's important to avoid going through the motions but comprehend and embrace the values they represent. We should love the Lord with all our heart, soul, mind, and strength, understanding that our faith takes personal action, not just 20 minutes of our life.

Unfortunately, many people of all ages go out and plan a baptism without taking the time to truly understand the importance of developing a much-needed relationship with God. Meanwhile, they disregard the complete spiritual relationship for their entire lives, assuming everything is fine and dandy. People often fail to acknowledge that the whole process is a humble step toward accomplishing their spiritual quest while adhering to Jesus' example. Meagan's approach was terrific in taking the time to reflect and study commitment.

## God's Strict

In Matthew 7:21-23, Jesus says, "Not everyone who says to me, Lord, Lord, will enter the kingdom of Heaven, but only the one who does the will of my Father who is in Heaven. Many will say to me on that day, Lord, Lord, did we not prophesy in your name and drive out demons and perform many miracles in your name? Then I will tell them plainly, I never knew you. Away from me, you evildoers!"

This serves as a reminder that faith in Jesus is not just a matter of words or actions but maintaining a genuine relationship. Everyone is hungry for God's love, goodness, and salvation. People are quick to demand many things from the Lord in some selfish ambition. It's not about me, me, me, I,

I, I, but about giving our actions, praise, thoughts and relationships to Jesus. When we depend on God, He'll provide us with joy to act upon our desires to please Him.

God's Word is clear on other humanistic topics, especially with people's loss of focus. I want you to seriously evaluate your faith and discover if anything I'm unfolding strikes a nerve or goes against your current understanding.

There's only one mediator between God and mankind, and His name is Jesus.

There's only one God.

Praying to and worshiping the deceased prophets, other humans, disciples, and idols isn't condoned. You are not to worship angels; even the angels will prohibit it. Praying to anything other than God, Jesus, Holy Spirit is regarded as idolatry, which is forbidden.

Jesus has risen from the grave, proving there's life after this.

God is a jealous God who desires to be first in our lives. Anything that takes precedence over Him, whether relationships or possessions, is uncalled for. This includes valuing anything above our relationship with God, such as family, professions, or other beliefs. God insists on being the highest priority in our lives and doesn't tolerate being second place. God has never planned on sending anyone to hell. If anyone ends up there, it's because of their own free will. God has done everything in His power to prevent this from happening, including sending His one and only Son to die on the Cross for you.

When you were created, you were given the free choice to live for or reject God, and despite anything you do, God will still love you. There's neither Jew nor Greek, there is neither slave nor free, there is no male and female, for you're all one in Christ Jesus. The Son of Man came to serve, not to be served. Be cautious of anyone who tries to rule over faith or have power over this dominion. Fake leaders will display and exercise authority over other beliefs and even governments.

When Jesus was crucified on that Cross, He took on the judgment and became guilty of every single sin that anyone has ever faced. Jesus bore the punishment of hell that each of us rightfully deserved. Just as God has forgiven us, we are called to forgive others. It can be challenging to release hurt and anger, but forgiveness is paramount.

# Embracing Faith Amidst Adversity

Remaining steadfast in our faith and aligning ourselves with God's purpose can be challenging amidst adversity. It becomes imperative to navigate our thoughts and emotions skillfully to maintain our spiritual connection. This involves consciously fostering optimism and seeking out moments of gratitude and contentment. By shifting our perspective toward hope and expressing appreciation, we can weather inevitable doubts and fears, viewing trials as avenues for personal growth and deepening our faith. Through life's challenges, we uncover resilience and fortify our hearts.

To nurture our spirit, it's essential to invest time in studying, reflecting, and actively building our relationship with God. Addressing unhealthy habits isn't solely God's responsibility; it's an opportunity for personal growth. Patience isn't merely granted but learned through practice. While God's blessings bring joy, true happiness stems from how we choose to invest our time and energy. In moments of pain or suffering, God's grace proves sufficient to carry us through, drawing us nearer to Him by distancing us from worldly distractions. As God shows His love for us, our reflection of that love brings Him joy in our faithfulness.

Understanding the true essence of faith demands persistent effort toward growth and knowledge acquisition. Finding meaning and contentment necessitates a strengthened connection with the divine, actively engaging in our spiritual journey. Community and camaraderie play pivotal roles in embracing and walking along God's intended path. Within these bonds, individuals flourish, drawing strength from both God and fellow believers. Scripture teaches that Christians function as a unified body, each contributing uniquely. Utilizing study groups for connection and fellowship expands beyond self-discovery.

In today's interconnected world, technology has revolutionized the formation and maintenance of spiritual communities. Platforms like social media offer valuable avenues for Christians to connect with like-minded individuals and forge new support systems. Through online forums and groups, believers share personal stories, provide mutual support, and engage in meaningful discussions about faith, transcending geographical barriers. Engaging respectfully in these virtual communities broadens our perspectives, challenging preconceptions and deepening our understanding of truth.

Such interactions promote peace, tolerance, and harmonious coexistence, enriching our spiritual journey in this digital age. However, it's crucial to acknowledge the internet's pitfalls. Some misuse these platforms for social bullying, tarnishing reputations, and causing harm. Therefore, while embracing the benefits of online connectivity, we must vigilantly guard against negative influences, striving to uphold principles of kindness, respect, and empathy in all interactions.

Moreover, in a time when defending our faith is increasingly important, many Christians hesitate to publicly display their inner strength. This hesitation leaves believers feeling isolated or unsure about navigating discussions on their beliefs. Yet, standing firm in our faith and confidently articulating our beliefs, both online and offline, is vital. This not only fortifies our personal decisiveness but also serves as hope in a world in need.

Defending our faith with grace, humility, and wisdom can initiate meaningful dialogue and foster understanding among individuals with diverse perspectives. Therefore, while embracing the positive aspects of online communities, we must also affirm our faith when faced with challenges or opposition. Everyone has the right to free speech, even when it challenges personal beliefs. Embracing diversity in socioeconomic status, gender, race, or ethnicity doesn't restrict God's plan. Reflecting God's heart, we reveal His unfailing love by creating environments that welcome and value individuals from all backgrounds. Diversity enriches our perspective and enhances our understanding, facilitating growth and deeper learning about our faith.

As we explore this significance, let's examine the importance of spiritual accountability and the impact of supporting others within the body of Christ. Our growth as believers hinges on our accountability to God. Surrounding ourselves with fellow Christians who can hold us responsible fosters honesty, openness, and support, motivating us to align with God's purpose and keep focused on His plan. Engaging with reliable individuals who challenge and guide us heightens awareness of our actions, guiding us toward spiritual growth and accountability.

Merely believing in God isn't enough; our lives and actions must reflect change. Living as followers of Christ should be our focus, not living for worldly desires. Matthew 10:32 reminds us, "Therefore, everyone who confesses Me before men, I will also confess him before My Father who is in Heaven. But whoever denies Me before men, I will also deny him before My Father who is in Heaven." As Christ's followers, we strive to demonstrate God's love and compassion, being the salt and light of the world. Reflecting Jesus's teachings, we fulfill our mission as His disciples by advocating for justice, serving our communities, and aiding those in need.

The Apostle Paul stressed the importance of serving others with humility and love, contributing to the well-being of our community. Strengthening bonds within our faith community through service impacts lives positively. Faith transcends church walls or formal gatherings; it permeates every aspect of our lives. Whether at home, work, or among friends, we manifest God's love through actions and interactions.

James 1:22 urges us, "But be doers of the word, and not hearers only, deceiving yourselves." This verse compels us not merely to listen to God's Word but to actively live out our faith through actions. Again, believing isn't enough; we must apply our faith daily and honor God through our deeds.

I recall a lesson my grandfather taught me as a child: "You can lead a horse to water, but you can't make him drink." Regardless of socioeconomic status, gender, race, or ethnicity, God's plan isn't limited. Reflecting God's heart and demonstrating His love create environments that welcome and embrace all people. Diversity enriches our perspective, fostering growth and deepening our understanding of faith.

## The Necessity of Worshiping with Others

As loving people, we naturally crave connection and interaction with one another. This social nature extends to how we express our beliefs and engage in acts of worship. Praying for each other and reading the Bible together hold immense reinforcement and inspiration. In these shared experiences, we learn from one another, share our stories, and offer support during life's challenges.

Gathering with others to praise and worship God reflects both unity and humility. It allows us to affirm our shared beliefs and recommit to living according to our faith's principles. Participating in communal worship benefits not just individuals but the entire church body. It fosters a sense of belonging, helps us uncover meaning and purpose, and provides the support needed to publicly practice our faith.

In today's fast-paced world, finding a spiritual community where we can connect and contribute is invaluable. Whether attending church, joining a small group, or participating in a prayer circle, there are various ways to share life with others and enhance our worship experience. Try different churches and find one that provides the support and encouragement you need. Many churches broadcast online, which is a great way to understand how each service operates before a personal visit.

Being part of a spiritual service can make navigating life's challenges more manageable. In difficult stretches, it's common to feel disconnected and isolated. However, being part of a community reassures and motivates, helping us maintain resilience and hopefulness. Worshiping with others aids spiritual growth, especially when singing with a choir. Great music becomes magical when all voices are carried throughout the building.

During a church service, singing with everyone else, voices lifted in praise, creates a unique moment of profound spiritual connection. As the music resonates through the sanctuary, something extraordinary happens within the hearts of those gathered. It's a moment when our defenses, emotional barriers, and personal walls come crashing down, laid bare before God. In that sacred space, if we allow ourselves to be vulnerable, God reaches out and touches us where we stand. His presence becomes discernible, surrounding us with peace and love that transcends our understanding.

In those precious moments, all pretense fades away, and we are left in awe of His majesty and grace. It's a moment of surrender, of opening our hearts to His embrace, and allowing His transformative power to work within us. Through the beauty of music and worship, God offers healing, renewal, and an overwhelming sense of His unconditional love. From song to sermon, you'll have this internal joy you look forward to week after week.

Searching for a good church home can be challenging if you don't already have one. You must keep looking until you find a community of people with whom you can connect and feel supported. This search requires patience. Remember, developing genuine connections with other Christians, like any relationship, requires time and effort. The advantages of being part of a community of believers will transform your life completely.

Feel free to explore the various ways to worship God in a group setting. Let yourself enjoy the excitement of getting your blessings each week. Worshiping God in a community will enable us to become more intimate with God. When we meet to pray, sing, and study the Bible, we invite the Holy Spirit to come and dwell among us, and we allow God to work in our thoughts and hearts.

Following Jesus' resurrection, He left the Holy Spirit, also known as the Helper, with every believer who accepted Him as their Lord and Savior. However, not everyone is accustomed to praying with the Holy Spirit, so being surrounded by other believers is essential. Since we're all fallen, we need all the help we can get. If we were perfect Christians, we wouldn't need a Savior. But since everyone needs Jesus, the church is a hospital for sinners.

In pursuing God's will, it's paramount to be available, seek His guidance, and submit to His authority. Our understanding of God's plan strengthens when we're connected to fellow Christians. If you're feeling lost and uncertain about your path, reaching out to others for guidance and support can be incredibly enlightening. In the end, you'll realize that true happiness and fulfillment come not from what we achieve but from the relationships we cultivate with others.

Central to the Christian faith is the act of worship, which underscores our devotion to God. Worship isn't solely an individual practice but a collective one, highlighting unity with shared experiences. Throughout history, collective worship has been a cornerstone of any spiritual practice, from the gatherings of the Old Testament to Jesus with His disciples. Communal worship helps us understand God better by incorporating diverse perspectives.

Participating in combined worship offers numerous benefits, enriching both individuals and the community. It expands our knowledge of God, deepening our understanding of His attributes and greatness. Moreover, it provides a supportive environment where believers can connect and feel welcomed. This collective experience strengthens our faith and motivates us to be the best we can be. While moments of solitary worship may be necessary, communal prayer reminds us that we are part of something greater, a unified family.

# Leaders of the Church

It's disheartening to see how some people resort to violence against preachers simply because of their financial status. Remember, God sees the heart and intentions of a person, not their material possessions. As long as people come to God and worship, that should be the main focus. Judging someone based on their finances or way of life is not our place. Each preacher or minister receives a percentage based on their church income. We should focus on our own journey of faith and strive to build a relationship with God. If someone has an issue with a particular preacher or church, they are free to open up their own church and spread their message. We should always strive to be kind and understanding toward others and avoid resorting to violence or hateful behavior.

It's interesting to note that while some preachers preach for free, others run businesses or have their own Bible versions. Many vary in income based on church membership or tithes. Some preachers believe that preaching should be done for free or with bare minimum donations, as it's a calling from God. On the other hand, some preachers think they should be compensated for their work, just like any other profession. This compensation can come in the form of a salary or from selling books, videos, or other materials related to their ministry. Ultimately, the decision of how to conduct their ministry and finances is up to each preacher and can vary greatly depending on their circumstances.

## The Importance of Being in A Bible Study

When we pray together, our voices and intentions merge, creating a powerful synergy that strengthens our petitions. The group's collective focus and energy lead to higher spiritual fulfillment and a deeper connection to God. We cultivate a strong sense of connectivity and compassion as we pray for one another's needs, fostering a loving and hospitable congregation. Each of us should pray for the lost as Heaven rejoices over a single soul saved. We must carry our faith into our daily lives, standing up for Christ even when it's unpopular or when others may mock us. Sharing our thoughts and beliefs with others is essential for spiritual growth. Engaging in discussions or study sessions with fellow believers offers new interpretations and a deeper comprehension of God's Word. Each person brings a unique perspective, enriching our spiritual understanding and motivating us to share our faith and grasp the essence of faithfulness through the ages.

Group Bible study prepares us for life beyond the church walls, uniting people from diverse backgrounds, ages, and professions into a community of believers. This diversity showcases the richness of God's creation and emphasizes acceptance of everyone. Engaging with individuals who have different perspectives and life experiences enhances our understanding of God's intentions and encourages us to appreciate each person's unique qualities. Through these interactions, we delve into the chapters and details of the Bible, using and sharing our spiritual gifts—whether through prayer, song, or service—to uplift and strengthen each other.

By collaborating in Bible study, we work together to fulfill God's mission and improve the lives of those around us. Having a supportive network of fellow believers provides comfort, guidance, and inspiration during times of need. Sharing our struggles and seeking advice from others offers perspective and reassurance that we are not alone on our journey. The collective wisdom and support of the community empower us to overcome obstacles and remain steadfast in our faith. Through mutual encouragement, we find the strength and resilience to navigate life's trials while maintaining our commitment to God.

Bible study allows us to expand our knowledge, gain a deeper understanding of the Scriptures, and see how they relate to our daily lives. For many, Bible study is the primary way they are spiritually nourished. Participating in a group study helps establish a routine of regular Bible reading and reflection. As we deepen our understanding of the Bible, we cultivate greater reverence and respect for it. Frequent reading and meditation on the verses strengthen our relationship with God, reminding us of His plans and promises. Regular Bible study meetings provide numerous benefits, including increased familiarity with the Bible, spiritual maturity, stronger relationships with other Christians, and a consistent study routine.

Engaging in a Bible study also offers valuable accountability. During difficult times, we can rely on our church family for support and motivation, helping us stick to our study schedules. As we explore the Bible together, we encourage each other to live out its principles, fostering a more loving and compassionate community. Shared study and reflection provide insights into dealing with life's stresses and challenges. Biblical teachings on forgiveness, gratitude, and humility help us cultivate a positive mindset even amidst hardship. Studying Jesus' life and teachings on compassion and empathy inspires us to be kinder and more understanding toward others.

Various Bibles are available, including study editions, chronological versions, and others tailored to different needs. While it's crucial not to alter the inspired Word of God, having access to the Bible in any form is better than not having it at all. When choosing a Bible study group, consider their unique approaches and focuses. Some groups may center on specific doctrines or follow the preacher's message, while others prioritize creating a supportive environment for studying Scripture. Participating in a Bible study involves group interpretation and shared wisdom, enriching our comprehension of Scripture and its significance in our daily experiences. This collaborative learning environment fosters community and mutual encouragement among believers on their faith journey. Finding a community that expands your mindset and encourages spiritual growth and meaningful discussions is vital. You should want to be involved.

The support we offer each other in Bible study motivates us to apply biblical teachings and assist one another when needed. This shared responsibility fosters spiritual growth and strengthens our practice of sharing personal testimonies and experiences with God. Each member's unique journey contributes to the collective wisdom and inspiration within the group, serving as a powerful reminder of God's transformative grace and encouraging others in their faith walk. Engaging in respectful dialogue, seeking guidance from trusted resources, and collaborating on interpretations deepen our understanding of God's Word, developing a richer appreciation for the depth and complexity of Scripture through collective study and reflection.

As I stated in a previous chapter, I take a three-tiered approach to helping others study the Bible, which allows people to understand its vast amount of information.

Level 1 is geared toward those new to Christianity and seeking an introduction to the faith. It covers the basics of developing a relationship with God and understanding the core beliefs.

Level 2 is focused on delving deeper into the Scriptures and learning about Jesus and His teachings. This level involves reading through the compiled letters and statements in the Bible and understanding the principles and values central to the Christian faith.

Level 3 is the most advanced and is intended for those interested in exploring the Bible's deeper, more complex aspects. This involves uncovering the hidden meanings and prophecies in the text. Understanding the roles of angels and their purposes and the workings of Heaven. Researching the Book of Revelations and the complex interplay between various elements of the end times.

# Spiritual Gifts

As outlined in the Bible, spiritual gifts encompass various abilities bestowed upon believers by the Holy Spirit to enlighten the church and serve others. These gifts include but are not limited to healing, wisdom, knowledge, discernment, faith, miracles, prophecy, and interpretation of tongues. Wisdom entails a deep understanding of God's will and the ability to apply divine principles to life situations. Knowledge involves insights into spiritual truths and Scripture, aiding in teaching and guiding others.

Faith enables believers to trust God wholeheartedly. Healing and miracles manifest through prayer and divine intervention, bringing physical, emotional, and spiritual restoration. Prophecy entails delivering messages from God for encouragement, edification, or correction. Discernment allows individuals to distinguish between truth and falsehood, guiding them in making righteous decisions. Tongues and interpretation of tongues involve speaking in other languages under the Holy Spirit's influence and deciphering these messages for the church's instruction.

These spiritual gifts collectively empower believers to minister to others, build up the body of Christ, and glorify God through their service and obedience. Each person has particular talents and skills that can benefit the community. We may help the community develop and edify by actively engaging in worship services, whether by leading prayers, singing, serving, or conversing. We can all work together to fulfill God's mission and share our gifts in a spirit of cooperation, empowerment, and support for one another.

These spiritual gifts can be hindered or suppressed by attitudes and actions contrary to the Holy Spirit's leading. Additionally, there are examples in the Bible where individuals who once used their spiritual gifts seemed to have lost their effectiveness or connection due to disobedience or lack of faith. Whether this constitutes a permanent loss of spiritual gifts, or a temporary hindrance is a matter of debate among Christian scholars. Ultimately, the Bible emphasizes the importance of nurturing and using spiritual gifts faithfully, acknowledging that they are given by God for the benefit of the body of Christ.

# Reality Check

To lead a meaningful and fulfilling life, it's vital to understand God and allow Him to shape your character. Your faith can guide you toward a life that's purposeful and abundant in meaning. Everyone needs to take time for self-reflection and evaluate their views. The concept of faith may differ from person to person, but it can profoundly impact how we navigate life's challenges. It allows us to find direction, purpose, and hope, all crucial elements in living intentionally.

Although religion and faith are often used interchangeably, faith is commonly understood as the firm belief in a divine being or a higher power. Let us examine some situations to recognize the present condition of our world. We live in a time of turbulence, where people feel anxious and uncertain due to various issues such as political instability and economic insecurity. It's not uncommon to feel stuck or lost in one's personal development.

Many individuals experience moments of hesitation where they question their life's purpose and direction. Faith can be challenging to navigate, and it's okay to occasionally feel like you've lost your enthusiasm because we're all human. If you've ever wondered where you're heading, know you're not alone; many others have experienced these emotions. Give yourself time to reflect and assess your life. Embrace the journey, take it one step at a time, and trust the process.

Reflect on questions related to your beliefs, aspirations, and priorities can be a practical approach to gaining clarity and direction. Taking the time to ponder these topics can deepen your understanding of your motivations and the outcomes you wish to achieve. For instance, you could evaluate whether your pursuits align with your environment or are consistent with the kind of person you aspire to be. By engaging in reflective practice, you can enhance your self-awareness and discover whether your life choices are self-guided or divinely inspired.

Trust is a critical aspect of personal growth. It entails accepting your ability to achieve everything God has intended for you. Strengthening your faith is essential to achieving your goals and overcoming any obstacles that may come your way. Following Jesus' examples and teachings could help you stay on track. Conducting a reality check requires acknowledging both your strengths and weaknesses. This allows you to confront the realities of your current situation, including your choices and current direction. It acts as a wake-up call, prompting you to reevaluate your assumptions, ideals, and objectives and make necessary changes to align them with God's desired results.

I want you to consider whether living a Christian life is difficult for you. So many of us would rather live however we wish. Obeying Biblical teachings involves changing your lifestyle to follow Christ. If you don't feel living the Christian life is hard, you aren't trying. Living and walking in the light is impossible without the power of God. We need to believe what the Bible says in order to have righteousness in God's eyes.

A reality check comes when you reflect on how deeply your beliefs shape your choices, actions, and overall perspective. By examining your thoughts and behaviors, along with their impact on your life, you can identify areas where your faith might need renewal. There will be moments of doubt or uncertainty, and while these can be unsettling, they also present opportunities for growth. Instead of viewing doubt as a weakness, embrace it as a catalyst for deeper exploration and understanding. It drives you to seek answers, engage in meaningful conversations, and venture toward spiritual enlightenment.

You might discover that your faith has become stationary or estranged from a healthy relationship with the Lord. This insight shouldn't depress you; instead, it should inspire you to rekindle your spirit. You can restore your faith and re-establish your connection to its meaning by turning to books, trustworthy mentors, or practices like prayer and meditation. Spot any discrepancies or contradictions between your behavior and the faith you claim to have. It challenges you to consider whether your actions are consistent with the teachings of Jesus or if you prefer ignoring a Holy God and living out your selfish ways. This self-awareness gives you the power to make the necessary changes and take accountability for your actions. You must ensure that your faith is more than just a static set of assumptions. By accepting the realities of your current situation and actively seeking spiritual maturity, you can embark on a path of personal transformation. It's time to live a life of profound purpose and confidence.

## Your Present State

When assessing your spiritual path, it's critical to be completely truthful with yourself and give yourself the benefit of honesty. This assessment calls for evaluating your spiritual life and where you are right now. It's natural to feel that you're doing well on your own and you feel good where you are. Actively pursuing God and making progress is the single most essential aspect. Remember Leviticus 22:31: "Therefore you shall keep my commandments and do them: I am the Lord."

Never forget that God loves you and has a purpose for your life, regardless of where you are in your spiritual path. Have faith that He will steer you in the correct direction and provide for all your needs. It's so simple to become preoccupied with the mundane activities of daily life that we frequently fail to take a break and refocus. When was the last time you allowed yourself to relax, take deep breaths, and assess your spiritual well-being? How knowledgeable of God would you say you are? Have you experienced any significant progress lately, or do you feel like you're currently stuck in one place? The responses to these questions aren't easy but necessary; we must be honest about our feelings.

Don't give up hope even though you feel like you're drifting further away from God. There's never a time when it's too late to ask for forgiveness and request His presence. He's always there, waiting for us with his arms wide open. Jesus left the Holy Spirit with us; always be willing to pray with the Spirit anytime you need assistance. Even when you don't know how to pray, ask the Spirit for advice and wisdom.

How would you describe the state of your connection with God at this point? Do you make it a habit to pray and study the Bible regularly? Do you have a strong network of loved ones and friends who can provide spiritual support and challenge you? When assessing where you are on your spiritual journey, realize it takes effort to maintain a relationship. In Matthew chapter 7, Jesus warns about the importance of doing God's will and not just professing your faith.

When life is over, you don't want to hear the words, "Depart from me; I never knew you."

The Apostle James stated faith without action is lifeless. This verse highlights how crucial it is to put our faith into practice. It serves as a reminder that our views should be displayed through our actions and decisions, actively influencing our lives and those around us. We evaluate the consistency between our beliefs and deeds to ensure our faith is strong and alive.

As you assess the state of your relationship with God, consider how your faith affects your choices, attitudes, and relationships. Are you actively forgiving people, exercising love and compassion for others, or are you seeking justice? Consider opportunities to show kindness, assist others, and positively impact the world. Let your faith act as a catalyst for development and improvement.

To enhance your connection with God:

Conduct a reality check by evaluating areas that require improvement and broadening your understanding of God's intentions.

Consider incorporating spiritual practices into your daily routine, such as how you plan on integrating worship into your life.

Take time to explore various resources that can help you gain a deeper understanding of the Bible.

Seek the support of others who can provide you with motivation, guidance, and a sense of community.

Reality checks intend to spur growth and revive your zeal to find God's purpose rather than depress or overwhelm you. Evaluate your motives, make sure your actions reflect your values, and take deliberate action to develop a closer relationship with God. Take advantage of this opportunity to evaluate your situation and make any required corrections.

Consider the character traits essential to your faith, such as compassion, forgiveness, patience, and thankfulness. Think how successfully you live out these characteristics every day. Are there instances where you could be more forgiving or compassionate to others? By evaluating your personal growth or the lack thereof, you can identify opportunities for improvement and become more motivated to actively enhance these qualities in your interactions.

Self-reflection can help you identify behavior patterns and habits that might impede your spiritual development. Do you have bad habits or unhealthy attachments that prevent you from achieving your spiritual objectives? How do you handle difficulties and disappointments? Do you perceive challenges as chances for improvement and try to learn from them, or do they discourage and slow you down?

Everyone's path is unique, so it's best to avoid comparing yourself to others. Instead, focus on yourself. Criticizing others is counterproductive when we should concentrate on the person in the mirror. Personal progress necessitates endurance, acceptance of change, and patience. Embrace the transformational power of your faith and personal growth, understanding that every step you take will bring you closer to God's plan for your life. As you actively seek progress on your spiritual journey, trust in His wisdom and grace and stay open to the opportunities that come your way.

## Abraham and Sarah

There was a time in the Old Testament when Abraham was 75, and Sarah was 65 years old. God told Abraham he would have a child. Both were senior in their years to bear children, but God promised descendants. Abraham believed in God and waited 15 years until he was 90, and there were still no children. Sarah outlined a plan for Abraham to have a child with a servant, and then, they would finally have offspring. They agreed on "their" terms versus God's plan and eventually had a son outside their marriage.

Ten years later, Abraham and Sarah couldn't believe it; they had a son whom they named Isaac. They were very proud, and Isaac thereafter became the father of Jacob, whom

God renamed Israel, and later became the grandfather of the twelve tribes of Israel known as the Israelites.

It's natural to think we know what's best for ourselves, but there's beauty in surrendering to God's divine timing. While we strive for specific outcomes, certain plans beyond our comprehension are already laid out.

# Trials

Trusting in God's timing can be difficult, especially when faced with setbacks or delays that can be frustrating and discouraging. However, obstacles may be intentional and part of a bigger plan we are unaware of. The Bible lists many examples of trials and tribulations, and through their faith and trust in God, they overcame their challenges and emerged stronger.

The story of Joseph in Genesis is a legend of resilience and perseverance in the face of adversity. Despite being sold into slavery by his own brothers, Joseph worked hard and remained faithful to his beliefs, ultimately rising to a position of power in Egypt. Even when unfairly imprisoned, Joseph never lost hope or gave up on his dreams. In the end, his unwavering faith and determination paid off, as he was able to use his position to save his family and the surrounding regions from famine. Joseph is a testament to the power of hope, faith, and perseverance and inspires all who face difficult times.

In the Book of Job, we see a man who endures incredible suffering and loss as God allows Satan to test Job to his very limits. Since God is sinless and full of glory, He couldn't perform the act. It's believed that angels and fallen angels among us are limited in their abilities and powers unless God allows it to happen. Yet, after everything that happened, Job lost all 10 of his children, his livestock, his wealth, his possessions, and his health, along with his closest friends. Job's wife encouraged him to curse God and die! Job remained faithful to God and was ultimately rewarded for his steadfastness.

There are several accounts in which Jesus is tempted and tested. One of the most well-known is when He is tempted by Satan in the wilderness for 40 days and nights. Satan offers Jesus food, power, and glory, but Jesus resists and responds with Scripture, saying, "Man shall not live by bread alone, but by every word that proceeds out of the mouth of God." Another instance is when Jesus is tested by the religious leaders of His day, who try to trap Him with their questions. However, Jesus always responds with wisdom and truth, overcoming His critics and demonstrating His authority over anything that comes His way.

We can see that even though Jesus faced trials and temptations, He overcame them through His faith and obedience to God. Jesus handed Himself over to be crucified for humanity. So, while it may be challenging to understand the purpose of delays or setbacks, we can take comfort in knowing there's a bigger picture to unfold. We can all learn from Genesis to the New Testament that God tests His people. And through your moments, you'll discover whether you turn to God for help or use your own judgment.

Were these other encounters intended to be recorded for posterity so that we can learn from the best scenarios?

Are they characteristics of a strong, unwavering faith?

You betcha!

## Lukewarm

In the Book of Revelations, chapter 3 states, " I know your deeds, that you are neither cold nor hot. I wish you were either one or the other! So, because you are lukewarm, neither hot nor cold, I am about to spit you out of my mouth." This passage underscores the importance of being committed to our faith and actions rather than being indecisive or lukewarm.

When I was young in my faith, around the age of 17, a coworker named Vien invited me to church, and on the third invite, I decided I'd attend. I explained my lifestyle to my Sunday school group. Prayer wasn't always a part of my routine, but I found myself turning to it in times of dire need. I believed in God, but my life didn't involve reading the Scriptures or a daily walk with God. I kept my ears open and soon learned that God doesn't tolerate fence riders; you're either for or against Him.

Are you living for your own gratification, or are you living to serve the Lord your God?

Here are some vital facts. When we have delayed or partial obedience to the Lord, it equals disobedience. Our obedience is a natural outflow of our faith, demonstrating the authenticity of our faith. God doesn't plan to remove your disobedience but wants you to surrender your all to Him. He wants you to have faith that you can't live without, something valuable, worthwhile, meaningful, and steadfast dedication.

Giving yourself to the Lord is not a one-time decision; it's a continual decision. The world is full of temptations and distractions that can pull us away from our faith. That's why it's important to be mindful of our surroundings and the people we interact with, as they may or may not care about your soul. We must surround ourselves with people who support our faith and encourage us to stay on the right path. In doing so, we can continue to make the conscious decision to give ourselves to the Lord every day and strengthen our relationship with Him. Jesus suffered for our sins, those considering themselves righteous and the unrighteous, allowing the opportunity of salvation.

## God Requires Your Loyalty

Once upon a time, people sought after God in all their decisions and hopes for the future. Children were raised in a God-fearing household, understanding that God can make or break civilizations. Christians were viewed as the solution and contributors to the spreading of the gospel. But now, society loves living for themselves and has become selfish in many ways, and Christianity is just another option out of hundreds.

The Bible lists historical moments when cities were destroyed or conquered by other nations because of disobedience. You may ask why there aren't more people coming to Jesus or what's happening to our world. The better question is, when was the last time you shared your faith with someone else? Are you explaining to others how to get saved?

God has never sent an angel to witness to anyone. He sends His people to do that.

Every person needs to share their faith. Jesus requires commitment; if anyone claims to be a follower of Christ, they need to walk in their faith. One's faith shouldn't be sporadic and subject to personal desires and necessities. Rather, it should be a constant belief that is present at all times. God isn't something you take off the bookshelf once a year. He requires your attention. Many people don't attend church and have nothing to hold themselves accountable.

Some come to church on Sunday morning, trusting in God, and then forget about everything the very next day when Monday arrives. Jesus taught that you cannot have two masters, yet so many people look in all directions for answers. If you're putting your trust in your job, finances, best friend, worldly news, what the president said, or the lyrics of your favorite music artist, go do it and see what happens.

But if Jesus is your Lord, your God, then follow Him.

God will always expose your false hopes. When we seek material things, status, relationships, and social media accounts, they will all leave us empty and void. If you're married, don't expect your partner to fill you up with happiness; that's God's job. Your life here is temporary, and searching out your earthly alter will make you distracted and lost. Each of us needs to worship, find our holy place, repair the brokenness, and deepen the spiritual connection. It's not just about working harder to believe, but rather choosing wisely where you place your confidence.

You could have all the dedication in the world by believing in fake gods and idols and those individuals covering themselves with gold, claiming to be the most high. In the eyes of God, there is no hierarchy when it comes to our relationship with Him. Everyone can have a one-on-one personal relationship, regardless of social status, background, or accomplishments. God desires a personal relationship with each of us, and He invites us to come to Him as we are. We do not need to have any special credentials or qualifications. All we need is a humble and sincere heart to seek Him, and He will meet us right where we are. This personal relationship allows us to experience His love, grace, and mercy in a profound and intimate way. We can find comfort, guidance, and strength in His presence, and He can transform our lives from the inside out.

You have the capacity to believe in yourself so strongly that you don't need to depend on others. When we're healthy and strong, and life seems to be going smoothly, it's easy to believe we don't need God's help. We may feel self-sufficient and capable of handling everything on our own. However, this perception is flawed. We always need God's help, regardless of our circumstances. Life is unpredictable, and we never know what challenges we may face in the future.

Relying solely on our strengths and abilities can lead to arrogance and a false sense of security. Recognizing our dependence on God and seeking His guidance and support can help us navigate life's uncertainties with humility and wisdom. All of the faith in the world will fail you. But the faith of a mustard seed in the one true God will always be enough to rescue you. How long will it take until you seriously accept your position, place your trust in Jesus, and serve Him?

# Finding New Beginnings

Forgiveness is one of the most powerful tools in our spiritual arsenal, offering a path to freedom and a fresh start. Often, we think of forgiveness as something we do for others, but it's just as crucial to forgive ourselves. Holding onto resentment and anger is like carrying around a heavy backpack of emotional weight. It doesn't just wear us down; it also stops us from building stronger relationships and moving forward.

In the Christian faith, forgiveness is more than just a way to let go of the past; it's a demonstration that we trust God to guide us toward a brighter future. When we choose to forgive, we're choosing to let God heal the pain and suffering that's been holding us back. And even if it's not always easy, forgiving is worth it because it brings us one step closer to experiencing God's love and grace.

Forgiving others is an act of mercy, reflecting the same compassion God shows us every day. It's a reminder that we all make mistakes and that we all need forgiveness at some point. When we let go of grudges, we release ourselves from the chains of past hurts and open the door to a stronger connection with God. It's a liberating feeling, knowing that by forgiving, we're creating space for joy, peace, and healing.

God's unconditional love and mercy are always available to us, no matter how many times we stumble. He wants a relationship with each of us and is ready to forgive us, but our unwillingness to forgive others can put a barrier between us and God. Holding onto anger and refusing to forgive only robs us of the joy and peace we deserve.

Forgiveness doesn't mean forgetting or endorsing the wrongs done to us; it's about choosing to rise above and move forward with love and compassion. It takes real strength and courage to forgive, to say, "I won't let the pain in my past define me." It's a declaration that we're willing to follow God's lead and embrace His plan for our lives. Asking for forgiveness is a lifelong journey. It's about acknowledging our flaws, seeking God's guidance, and trusting that He's working to shape us into better versions of ourselves.

Imagine God as a master sculptor, standing before a block of raw stone. With each careful strike of the chisel, He shapes, refines, and brings to life a vision that only He can see. Just like an artist who crafts a beautiful sculpture from what seems like a formless rock, God works on each of us, gently removing the rough edges and smoothing out the imperfections. His artistry is patient and precise, revealing the beauty and potential that lie within us. As He chisels away the unnecessary and polishes the parts that need attention, we transform into unique masterpieces, expressions of His creativity and love. In God's hands, every strike of the chisel has a purpose, every scrape is intentional, and the final piece is a reflection of His divine craftsmanship. The process might be slow and sometimes uncomfortable, but the result is a breathtaking work of art, each detail carefully crafted to fulfill His perfect design.

When we forgive, we allow God to work through us, bringing His light into the world. Forgiveness is not a sign of weakness; it's a sign of strength. You can move forward with grace, let go of the burden of resentment, and invite God's love into your heart. Through forgiveness, you're opening yourself to transformation and allowing God to use you as an instrument of peace. By embracing forgiveness, you not only heal your heart but also deepen your relationship with God. This journey may not always be easy, but it leads to a life filled with love, compassion, and purpose. So, let's choose forgiveness and find the freedom it brings.

## God's Forgiveness and Grace

Many people trust in material possessions, believing "stuff" can provide security. But the "stuff" we own, actually ends up owning us. When we trust in God and seek His guidance, He forgives us and shows us unimaginable grace. If we don't, we might find ourselves lost, unable to fill the emptiness. Hebrews 11:1 states, "Faith is the assurance of things hoped for, the conviction of things not seen." Faith is the cornerstone of Christian life, and it means believing that God has a plan for us, even when we can't see the road ahead.

In 1st John 1:9, If we confess our sins and ask for forgiveness, God is there to cleanse us from all unrighteousness. But we must also believe in ourselves, knowing we have the strength to turn away from our misdeeds. This isn't just about saying sorry and moving on; it's about a total transformation of heart and mind. God's grace isn't a free pass to live however we want. It's the power that helps us rise above our sins and walk in a way that honors Him.

When we give our lives to Jesus Christ, we receive the gift of eternal life. It's like getting a brand new start with a clean slate. Romans 3:23-24 tells us that while everyone has sinned and falls short of the glory of God, we can all be justified by

His grace through the redemptive work of Jesus on the cross. That means no matter how messed up things get, God can fix it. His grace has no limits, reaching out to meet us wherever we are and offering a path to restoration and renewal.

Asking God for forgiveness is more than just acknowledging our wrongdoings; it's about saying, "God, I'm ready to do things your way." It's a turning point, a moment when we open ourselves to His guidance. Forgiveness may seem tricky, especially when we've been deeply hurt, but it's one of the most liberating things we can do. It lets us drop the heavy baggage of guilt and resentment, clearing the way for God's love to pour in.

When we hold onto unforgiveness, we are building a wall. Not only does it keep us from experiencing true peace and joy, but it also makes it harder to hear His voice and feel His presence. Remember, God's grace is like an open door; it welcomes everyone, no matter how far they've wandered. All He asks is that we turn back to Him, repent, and accept His love.

God loves transformation. It's not a band-aid for our sins; it's a way to live a new life. 2 Corinthians 12:9 reminds us that God's grace is sufficient, and it's in our weakness that His power is made perfect. This is where we find true strength when we lean into God's grace and let Him work through us.

The key to understanding God's forgiveness is to remember that it's not about earning it.

Titus 3:5 tells us that we aren't justified by our own righteous works but by God's grace. And 2cd Peter 3:9 says that God isn't slow in keeping His promise; He's just patient, waiting for everyone to repent. So, whether you've just begun your journey of faith or deep into it, know that God's grace is there for you. It's the ultimate invitation to let go of the past and embrace a future filled with hope and purpose. If you're struggling, remember that forgiveness is always within reach; ask, and you'll find God's loving arms open wide, ready to welcome you back.

## An Entitled Attitude

It's easy to fall into the trap of thinking we deserve something without putting in the effort, but that's not the kind of life we're called to lead as Christians. The Apostle Paul, in his letter to the Thessalonians, urged them to work diligently and avoid idleness. He knew that a life centered on hard work, responsibility, and self-sufficiency leads to spiritual and physical well-being. Paul encouraged the Thessalonians to lead a quiet life, focus on their responsibilities, and work with their hands so that they could earn the respect of others and not be a burden on anyone.

This mindset keeps us grounded and focused on the things that matter.

Living with an entitled attitude can derail us from our Christian journey in many ways. For one, Christianity emphasizes humility and serving others. If we start to believe we're owed something without giving back, we miss the point of our faith. An entitled attitude leads to a sense of superiority and the idea that we're more important than others. This can make us less empathetic and more likely to disregard the needs of those around us.

Moreover, entitlement can blind us from experiencing the complete picture.

We're called to be grateful for everything we have and to acknowledge the contributions of others. An entitled person takes these blessings for granted, acting as if they deserve them for no reason at all. This can create an atmosphere of ingratitude, where we forget to thank God and those who have helped us along the way. Entitlement can also undermine our sense of accountability and responsibility.

Christianity teaches us to own our actions and be accountable to everyone. Yet, when we feel entitled, we tend to blame others for our shortcomings and refuse to take responsibility. This leads to a cycle of excuses and a lack of personal growth. We should focus on living with humility, gratitude, and accountability to avoid these pitfalls. This means taking the time to appreciate what we have and recognizing that we are stewards of God's gifts. Instead of expecting special treatment, we should work hard and be willing to help. By doing this, we honor God's call to lead a life that uplifts others and brings glory to Him.

For example, consider volunteering in your community. By giving your time and effort to help others, you're contributing while grounding yourself in the Christian values of service and humility. Similarly, regularly practicing gratitude, whether through prayer, journaling, or simply thanking people, can help you stay focused on the blessings in your life and avoid taking them for granted. While it's easy to fall into an entitled mindset, living a Christian life represents being responsible.

## Direct Connection

Many people are looking for ways to build stronger relationships with the Almighty. The Bible is a great place to start, filled with wisdom and guidance. For instance, the prophet Jeremiah, who spoke for God, stated in Jeremiah 29:11, "For

I know the plans I have for you, plans to prosper you and not to harm you, plans to give you hope and a future." This verse reminds us that God's intentions are always for our good. If you feel lost, remember that He has a plan, and it's a great one.

Think of prayer as your direct line to God, a conversation where you can share your worries, dreams, and requests. It's a place where you can be yourself and trust that God is listening. Avoid practices that encourage praying to saints, angels, or departed humans. You have a direct connection, which allows you to communicate with God without intermediaries.

Many of us grew up attending catechism classes, where we were taught to pray to various saints, guardian angels, and Mary. It often seemed like these saints were intermediaries, as if God didn't have the time or the inclination to hear our prayers directly. In class, we were encouraged to seek the departed, almost as if our prayers would be more effective if channeled through these holy figures. Only Jesus is the Savior. Jesus is the one and only who bridges the gap between humanity and God. After all, every soul, upon departing from this world, returns to God.

Ecclesiastes 12:7 says, "Then shall the dust return to the ground it came from, and the spirit returns to God who gave it."

To clarify, all the Apostles, disciples, and all of our deceased family members from years past have returned to God. If you've ever felt awkward, as in someone or something has ever been watching you, it's not departed humans.

Moving on...

While saints are respected and honored for their exemplary lives and faith, they are not meant to replace or overshadow our direct communication with God. Praying to saints, while well-intentioned, can lead to a form of spiritual distraction. It implies that God is too distant or too busy to hear our prayers, which contradicts the teachings of Jesus about the nature of God's love and accessibility. The Bible encourages believers to pray directly to God. In Matthew 6:9-13, Jesus provides the Lord's Prayer as a model for how we should pray, addressing God directly as our Father. This direct line of communication is a vital aspect of our faith, fostering a personal and intimate relationship with our Creator.

You can pour out your heart and know that God, the Creator of the universe, hears you and responds to your prayers. Developing a strong relationship with God requires more than just reading Bible verses or praying when you need something. We need to adopt His guidance, even if it means stepping into the unknown or letting go of things we hold dear. It's a journey, not a sprint, and as you go, you'll find that God reveals Himself in beautiful and surprising ways. He becomes not just your Savior but also your friend and guide.

If you're looking for inspiration, check out these powerful verses:

Proverbs 3:5- 6: "Trust in the Lord with all your heart and lean not on your understanding. In all your ways, submit to Him, and He will make your paths straight."

Matthew 6:33: "But seek first His kingdom and His righteousness, and all these things will be given to you."

These two verses are like a GPS for your spiritual journey. They keep you on the right path. And remember, you don't have to do this alone. Surround yourself with a community of believers, join a Bible study group, or find a mentor. Hebrews 10:25 reminds us not to give up meeting together but to encourage each other. Strengthening your relationship with God involves practicing spiritual disciplines like prayer, Bible study, worship, and service. These practices aren't just religious rituals. They're ways to experience God's presence and understand His plan for your life. The more you engage in them, the closer you'll feel to Him.

So, take a step toward God today. Spend time in prayer, read the Bible, seek His guidance, and trust that He has a plan for you. The journey might be challenging, but the reward of a deeper, more meaningful relationship with the Almighty is worth every moment. Embrace it with energy, compassion, and an open heart, and you'll find the closeness you're looking for.

# Building a Faith That Endures

Maintaining faith can be challenging in a world where doubt and fear grapple with the mindset. Still, God encourages us to keep our faith strong, even in the face of trouble. Strengthening our faith is a continuous process that requires self-dedication, prayer, and commitment to the Lord. It's a journey that necessitates perseverance and effort, reminding us our faith is a personal responsibility. Although life isn't easy, even the most devout believers face struggles and doubts. Our shoulders weren't meant to carry the weight of the world.

People tend to neglect the spiritual aspects of life. A vast majority live each day according to their own will and without any consideration for God's teachings. If one is hesitant to express their faith for fear of offending others or disclosing their beliefs because they feel ashamed, they risk being rejected by God. Jesus once said, "If you deny me before others, I will deny you before my Father." That statement should change your life!

The Book of Revelations emphasizes the importance of wholehearted commitment, decisiveness, and consistency. The scripture highlights that some individuals who don't follow the Christian faith may seem indifferent and make jokes, even though they face the possibility of death and damnation. Some people are unsure whether it's worth believing in a Man who claims to be the Savior of their soul. According to the scripture, a day will come when the Lord will return. Nobody knows when this day will be. Despite this anticipation, we're told to remain faithful because the day is coming.

If you're a believer, you want to expand your faith beyond being a Sunday Christian; there are seven days a week. No matter how much you think you know, there's always more to discover about God's bigger plans. Engage in reading theological texts and researching how Biblical history ended up as it did. This constant learning keeps your faith dynamic and allows you to grow spiritually. Over 100 chapters discuss the end times and everything that leads up to that moment.

When you encounter difficulties, remember that God is always there. He's willing to guide you through every storm as long as you're ready. Read Job in the Old Testament and discover a strong man who refuses to give up. We might be tested to uncover our true thoughts and feelings. God acts according to His will, timing, and choosing, using whomever and however He sees fit.

Jesus came to serve, not to be served. All speculation will be shattered. Not all religions will lead to Heaven; Jesus never preached a religion. When He was born, He was humbled, later rejected, and crucified by the Romans. During His second coming, Jesus will be glorified. It won't matter if someone is a ruler, president, music artist, or sought-after social media professional. Every knee will bow, every tongue will confess Jesus is Lord.

You can depend on God, but you must rely on yourself. Work has always been God's plan. We are to be productive and contribute to our communities and our families. We need to be faithful in everything we do to avoid low self-worth. Forty days after Jesus' resurrection, He told everyone to go and make disciples and baptize them in the name of the Father, Son, and Holy Spirit. Nothing in life is free; salvation was paid for by the blood of Jesus.

God sees you and knows everything about your story, even the parts you try to hide from the world. He understands your pain, your struggles, and your fears. The beauty of having a loving God is that even though you may not see your story unfold. He has a plan for you; sometimes, your pain could be used for His glory. Every experience, whether good or bad, can be used to shape you into the person He wants you to be. Trust that God is in control and will work everything out for your good. Allow God to use your story to inspire and encourage others.

Sometimes, we're entrusted with tasks, and occasionally, we fall short. Failure is a natural part of life, and we may experience it repeatedly. However, bouncing back is essential for achieving success. If you've ever felt overwhelmed by your fears and thoughts, those mental images can materialize into actual outcomes. Mastering faith can help you eliminate fear from within.

## The Benefits of Your Faith

Demonstrating your beliefs and values affirms your faith and trust in God. While it's challenging to maintain focus during troubling times, it's a constant reminder that God is in charge and will never forsake you. No matter how difficult your circumstances may seem, stay strong when life feels like an uphill battle. You can conquer any mountain and emerge victorious.

We receive strength from an unlimited source, which will prevail over any challenge that stands in our way. In Deuteronomy, chapter 31, verse 6, God promises his people that he will never abandon or turn his back on them. We can always find peace regardless of the circumstances; God is there with us every step of the way.

God has countless ways of communicating with you. Whether in the Bible verses you read on each page or the Holy Spirit, who provides inspiration and creativity. He might bring someone into your life at the right moment to offer comfort or guidance, like a sign that you're not handling this alone. He can even speak to you in your dreams, offering insights and reassurance when you need it most. This constant presence and communication from God provide a sense of security, allowing you to face anything with renewed courage.

There are moments in our spiritual journey when we might feel that God is distant or not listening to our prayers. These times of perceived absence can be profoundly challenging, leaving us with a sense of loneliness and uncertainty. However, it is often during these moments of spiritual desolation that God is closest to us. His presence is not always felt through grand gestures or miraculous signs; sometimes, it's in the quiet, stillness, and seemingly mundane aspects of our lives that He works.

During these times, it's important to remember that God's silence does not equate to His absence. In fact, His quiet presence can be a powerful reminder of His faithfulness and love. Just as a parent watches over their child from a distance, allowing them to grow and learn, God's nearness is often felt in His silent support and unwavering presence. When we feel alone, it's an invitation to deepen our trust and faith, knowing that God is with us, guiding and sustaining us, even when we can't feel His presence directly.

## Persecution and Justice

Some individuals become discouraged when pressured or persecuted because they follow Jesus. Many people question why wicked people prosper, and those who do foolish acts don't get punished. There doesn't seem to be any justification or reward for following the Bible. The Apostle Paul tells everyone to stay faithful, and justice is coming. One day, the Lord will deal retribution to those who don't know God and those who don't obey the gospel. They will pay the penalty of eternal punishment.

Unbelievers might not pay the price in this life, but they will pay a higher price, which is understood as an eternal forfeit. This is well reflected in the Gospel of Matthew, where Jesus knew disbelievers and skeptics lived among the believers. Matthew 13:49 states how the angels will come and separate the wicked from the righteous and throw them into the blazing furnace, where there will be weeping and gnashing of teeth.

If you're someone who refuses to believe that a Holy God would do such a thing as banishment just because someone is a decent person and tries to do right most of the time, you'd be wrong. Many know about God but don't follow the commandments of His Son Jesus Christ. You either follow Jesus or refuse to do what He asks of you. We choose whether or not to have a relationship that will change our lives forever or reject the gospel. It's not Jesus who's pushing people away, but rather every person who chooses to walk away from Him.

Whoever you are, deep down inside, remember that God wants you to be great; He's already on your side. He desires you to have unbreakable faith. Cast aside the timidity, fear, and insecurity that wipes you out. We must be fearless; God wants us to take risks, be bold, and have bravery. Each of us needs to put on the full armor of God. The Bible lists several spiritual gifts, including discernment, wisdom, knowledge, faith, healing, miracles, prophecy, and interpretation. Jesus wants you to use your gifts in humility to benefit the body of Christ.

As a believer, the Spirit of God dwells within you, offering an unwavering source of comfort and solace for even the heaviest of burdens. His grace can lift this life's struggles, pains, and problems away. Sometimes, the ache we experience feels like it'll never end. Our time on Earth is short compared to eternity. Therefore, we must remember that everything in this life is momentary and brief. God will wipe away every tear, and soon, there will no longer be death.

By intentionally matching your actions with His will, you can be confident that you are seeking God's intentions for your life. Understanding the benefits of relying on your faith can open doors to a life filled with blessings, purpose, resilience, tranquility, and optimism. By investing in building relationships with those around you, you'll discover strength, direction, and a deeper connection with God. This connection will enrich your life in meaningful ways. There's nothing like networking and finding new best friends while expanding your horizons.

## Evolution to Space

There are over 1,000 religions and beliefs worldwide, and the one that impacts the education world is evolution. None of the main ideas of evolution have ever been observed. It states that everything we have today came from a single-cell organism that magically appeared from nothing. Evolution has different meanings.

Organic evolution is a scientific theory that explains how species change over time through natural selection and genetic variation. However, it should be noted that this theory will never explain how life originated from non-living matter. Despite extensive research and experimentation, scientists have yet to provide a definitive example of life arising from inanimate matter. While some people believe that natural chemical processes played a role in the origin of life, others hold the creation of the universe and all living things to God Almighty. The Bible states that God created the heavens and the Earth and provides a detailed chronology of events within the Bible if all choose to read.

Cosmic evolution is understanding where time, space, and matter come from. Many would express that we have three dimensions of physical space: length, width, and height. Educators have stated the fourth dimension is time, but time doesn't exist; it's just a unit of measurement. People love to comprehend their world, so time was invented. God doesn't have a watch; 1000 of our years is nothing compared to the biblical comprehension of eternity. Our fourth dimension is actually how there's gravity in space. Our planet has weight upon the universe, and it bends a small pocket in space that holds us in position. Since the moon is smaller than Earth, it cannot break free and fly away.

The fifth dimension refers to the unique, independent path each galaxy follows in the universe. Unlike objects within a single galaxy, which are influenced by each other's gravitational forces, galaxies themselves move along trajectories that are distinct from one another. For instance, planet Earth, situated in the Milky Way galaxy, follows an elliptical galactic path. If this path were a perfect circle, it would be simpler to comprehend. However, the complexity arises from the elliptical shape and the multitude of forces at play.

Our solar system, along with its confirmed planets, comets, and other celestial bodies, operates under the influence of gravitational forces. These forces govern the movement and interaction of objects within the solar system and the broader galaxy. The elliptical orbit of Earth, along with the gravitational interactions with other planets and celestial objects, creates a dynamic and ever-changing cosmic environment. Similarly, other galaxies also follow unique paths influenced by their own gravitational interactions, such as dark matter.

In my lifetime, there came a time when NASA could see 880 million light-years in all directions. But nowadays, we can see over 13 billion light-years. People have claimed to see alien life for hundreds of years. In fact, people all over the world claim to have seen visitors from who knows where. Given that we can observe billions of light-years in any direction, we would expect to see extraterrestrial life on the move.

From this science, I can realistically, religiously, and scientifically argue that extraterrestrial life doesn't exist. To reach our galaxy, solar system, and atmosphere, they would have to travel at the speed of light for millions of years, and we'd see them coming. Traveling at such speeds, they would inevitably crash into one of the massive meteors in the Milky Way galaxy and explode into pieces. They'd perish before any visitations could occur, not to mention the "sightings" and fabricated videos that arise annually.

In 1947, in Roswell, New Mexico, there was an incident in which people believed in an extraterrestrial spacecraft that crashed. Air Force Colonel Blanchard told the locals it was just a weather balloon. This earlier technology taught us how temperature and wind direction change at different altitudes. That's how civilian and military aircraft save time and fuel by flying with the wind rather than against it. Everyone wants to believe in something galactic and supernatural, but it's not an actual reality.

## Enduring Faith

Many people attribute the rise of atheism to the actions of Christians who claim to accept Jesus with their mouths but fail to reflect that acceptance in their lifestyle. This discrepancy between what they profess and how they behave can be a significant factor in why some individuals may question the validity of Christianity altogether. It highlights the importance of living your beliefs and values consistently and authentically.

The issue of hypocrisy among Christians can create a significant barrier for those who are questioning or exploring Christianity. If someone sees Christians who claim to follow specific values and beliefs but do not live them out, they may begin to doubt the authenticity of those beliefs. This can lead to a sense of disillusionment and skepticism about Christianity as a whole. For example, when people wear Christian clothes or a cross around their neck, it doesn't necessarily reflect that they are walking with God.

Everyone is prone to mistakes and shortcomings. Christians are not immune to anything and could easily struggle with living out their beliefs in their daily lives. We need to acknowledge our battles and strive to live a life that's consistent with God's desires. By doing so, we can demonstrate the authenticity and relevance of our faith to others. Recognize that Christianity is not just about following a set of rules or living up to certain expectations. It's about having a personal relationship with God and striving to love others as He loves us. This relationship is not always easy and requires ongoing effort and commitment.

Avoiding hypocrisy requires a humble and self-aware approach to life. Examine your actions and beliefs to ensure they align with Jesus' teachings. Acknowledge your weaknesses and work on improving yourself rather than pretending to be someone you're not. Practice what you preach. If you believe in something, then act on it. Avoid saying one thing and doing another, as this can create a sense of distrust and undermine your credibility. Be honest with yourself and others about your beliefs and values, and strive to live up to them every day.

## Enduring Families

It's no wonder so many families and marriages struggle. Besides climbing divorce rates and people trying to use each other, numerous lifestyles contribute to the challenges faced in relationships today. I've had to learn these lessons myself. One personal example is when you place your job before your spouse. Many of us work very hard to provide the necessities for our families. But once our jobs own us, we lose focus on the most important things. An employer can always find another employee, but you can't just go out and find another spouse.

Stereotypically, women can quickly put the children before their husbands. The importance of loving and caring for your family will always be there. The Bible states that a husband and wife become one flesh, and each person in the relationship needs to love and respect the other. There will come a day when all the children leave, and the nest will be empty. If you haven't worked on your relationship over the years, you will be complete strangers and have a broken marriage.

If you put your parents before your spouse, you'll hurt your marriage. The Bible says that a man will leave his father and mother and cleave to his wife. As each child grows up, they realistically leave their family to pursue one of their own. Parents are now considered extended family. When a man and woman love one another, they can't put each other first and cleave to one another if they haven't left their parents.

All marriages will suffer if you put yourself before your spouse. If two people try to use one another, there will be darkness and disrespect. If one is serving and the other takes advantage of it all, it'll feel like abuse, just like getting run over. When each person serves, loves, and cares for the other, it becomes a beautiful picture. God loves marriages; He created them. But God wants to be first in your marriage. When you love God with all your mind, heart, spirit, and strength first, He'll bless your household and strengthen your bond. As you love and serve each other as the biblical second devotion, everything will balance just right.

If any of you listening to or reading this still have a heavy heart about not being enough or not reaching your desired goals, please know that you are not alone. God's love for you is limitless, and He wants to give you everything; even the angels of heaven are envious of you. Jesus desires that you feel His love through His actions and sacrifices. Although He was here for 33 years teaching and healing all those around Him, Jesus was all about perfect timing, displaying humility, strength, and passion, giving everything He had to offer. The Holy Spirit was provided to give you the discernment and creativity to accomplish anything you wish. Jesus aspired to be the man you'd look up to. He wants you to shine bright and be all that you can be.

Without hesitation, Jesus laid everything on the line for you. Your safety, happiness, and relationship with Him mean more than you'll ever know. For many of us, that realization can bring tears. You're not just part of His life; you're His life, and He loves to see you smile. Remember, you're cherished beyond measure.

If you're interested in learning more about building solid relationships, grab a copy of The 8 Languages of Love and the Gems of Personality

From Amazon or listen to my Audible version narrated by Helpful Matthew, visit www.GarySPark.com for direct links.

# Prove It

Engaging in fruitful evangelism requires an understanding of the core doctrines of the Christian faith and genuine compassion for those with whom we share the message. It's essential to approach evangelism with a humble and open heart, recognizing that each person's journey is unique. By actively listening to others and seeking to understand their perspectives, we can effectively and respectfully address their questions and concerns.

Spreading the Gospel is not about winning debates or forcing our beliefs on others. Instead, we should convey the wisdom we possess or acknowledge our lack of it.

It's just like martial arts:

What is a black belt?

It's a white belt that didn't give up.

When answering someone or sharing your thoughts, if you encounter a question you don't know the answer to, let them know. Not everyone knows everything, so help them find someone who does.

The character of Jesus, His earthly mission, and how He exhibited love, compassion, and humility should be reflected in our words and deeds. Evangelism is not restricted to official contexts or organized approaches. Sharing personal testimony and having one-on-one talks are effective strategies. We must treat people's doubts, questions, or misunderstandings about Christianity with decency and love.

Building sincere connections creates an environment safe for conversation and enables others to witness the transformative influence of Christ. As prayer aligns our hearts with God's plans and makes way for divine appointments, evangelism becomes necessary when opportunities arise. By continually seeking His direction and asking Him to guide us to people who are open to the Gospel, we prepare ourselves to be effective instruments. We can also pray for those we're reaching out to, pleading with God to open their minds and soften their hearts to His truth.

Understanding that evangelism is a lifelong process necessitates ongoing learning and growth. We can better share the Gospel as we increase our knowledge of God's Word. Christian education, Bible study, and seeking mentorship from experienced believers can help us learn and better prepare us to handle the challenging issues that may arise during evangelistic interactions.

By adopting a holistic approach, we can carry out Jesus' charge to go into the world and proclaim the good news. May the Holy Spirit lead us to successfully share God's message of hope and salvation with a world in need. For us to effectively proclaim the good news and spread the Gospel, we need to be responsive to the Gospel message and attentive to the direction of the Holy Spirit. When sharing the hope we've found in Christ with others, we shouldn't try to impose our views on them by force; instead, we should be kind and courteous. When trying to show love by sharing the truth, we must be ready to address questions.

One can evangelize in several different ways; telling one's testimony or inviting another person to attend church could be the easiest way. You should pray for opportunities to share your faith, and it's equally essential to be prepared when those opportunities arise. The word of the Gospel must be protected from being watered down. The Gospel is evident when people understand the context of the verses.

Our ultimate objective should be to introduce others to Jesus Christ so that they can experience joy, freedom, and peace of mind, as everyone has an equal opportunity to be saved. The ability to communicate the Gospel's message to others is a blessing. We need to approach everything with a sense of appreciation for being part of God's family.

Firm believers frequently feel compelled to share their faith and educate others about it. Not everyone can dialogue, perform public lectures, or write articles for publication. New believers may feel uncomfortable discussing spiritual topics. That's why it's important to know where you are in your walk in order to share with someone else.

## Mandate of Making Disciples

If you're not already motivated, you'll be driven to share the hope that God has given you with the rest of the world. It's our job to spread the good news so that others can be saved. Mark 16:15 records that Jesus commanded his disciples to "go into all the world and preach the gospel." This verse was not a suggestion in any way, shape, or form; it was an absolute mandate. As Christians, we take this instruction seriously and do our best to follow it. Making disciples and evangelizing are two inseparable aspects of the same overall mission.

Making disciples involves teaching and nurturing individuals in their spiritual journey, helping them grow in their relationship with God and understanding the teachings of Jesus. Evangelizing, on the other hand, involves sharing the message of the Gospel with others and inviting them to embrace the Christian faith. Making disciples focuses on the ongoing growth and development of individuals. Evangelizing emphasizes reaching out to those who probably don't know the complete picture of the message. Both are essential for spreading the teachings of Jesus and bringing others into a meaningful relationship with God.

As a disciple of Jesus, it's both your responsibility and obligation to share the message of your faith with others. According to Acts 1:8, every Christian will receive power from the Holy Spirit to be His witness to the ends of the Earth. We need to ensure we're constantly ready to give an account for the hope that we have (1 Peter 3:15). Despite the depth of those Bible verses, the Gospel isn't hard to understand.

According to John 3:16, God sent Jesus Christ into the world to save those who had sinned against Him. This teaching is the core lesson that keeps repeating. Everyone's future will be determined by the choices they make. Sharing the good news about Jesus demonstrates His love for every person. Matthew 28:16–20 contains the Great Commission, which commands all Christians to proclaim that salvation is available to anyone who believes in Jesus Christ.

## Prove Jesus

Depending on who we're talking to, they might not believe in Jesus' existence or the miracles He performed. Others may want you to prove heaven is real or how anyone can be certain there's life after death. Some might desire a bigger picture: how is it true that our God exists?

In an earlier chapter, we've covered how history has documented Jesus' existence, so it's clear He was there. Nobody in their right mind would ever go to such lengths to profess Jesus has risen from the grave and that you could also have everlasting life by accepting Him as your Savior while actually believing a lie. We know the closest people to Him were willing to die for His cause. These Apostles truly believed in what they learned and everything they saw and experienced. After all, everything was documented in their lifetime; it's not like it was recorded by different people 1000 years afterward. These men walked, lived with, and experienced the life of Jesus.

They did everything without seeking fame or fortune. Humans don't dedicate their entire lives to anything unless it's necessary. They knew Jesus was real, He was serious, and every one of them needed to bring their A-game because history and salvation depended on it. Jesus performed many miracles; read all about them. Not one of them was selfish in nature. He was ready and available. He knew who had perfect faith, and those who believed knew if only they could touch His clothes, they'd be healed! Those around Him comprehended He wasn't like anyone else. Why would so many, strongly believe He was going to be the new King with power and authority? Everything documented from the Old Testament to the New Testament explained everything that was to happen for years to come, including the day Jesus rode down the hill on a donkey. Years and years of Scripture were recorded before any of these Apostles were alive, and yet everything came together like clockwork.

Jesus has always been reliable, from all the historical evidence to how He taught others to live, the importance of forgiving, and how He died and rose from the dead. He has credibility. When people request proof, it's usually because they haven't done any research for themselves or would rather have someone else explain the whole story. Nobody lives their lives on proof; we live by evidence.

The Bible is more than enough evidence as it lists everything that occurred, the years everyone lived, the rulers that reigned from Egypt to Europe to Asia, and anything else of importance. The civilizations that existed and those that were destroyed by fire and sulfur. The destruction and chaos of history have all been found in archaeological evidence. There's only one document that details as much chronology.

The evidence states God exists. Life comes from life; nothing comes from non-life. When you stare into the cosmos, there's intelligent design. People have knowledge and wisdom. We have free will. If we were nothing but a bunch of biochemical reactions, we wouldn't be free because we would already be determined to be a reaction. Each of us has the ability to think process logic; we already know what's right and wrong. We understand it's bad to kill or cause suffering. Why? Because God is love, and we are wired to Him. We can discuss and debate with others, unlike simple organisms. We have the capability to argue with ourselves and criticize ourselves when we're down. People abuse themselves, and sin can drive them to cause trouble for others. We judge ourselves and others. These abilities aren't mere biochemical reactions. There's more than meets the eye; we have a personality and a soul. We have free will that could only exist if there were a God.

## Ancient Beliefs and the Afterlife

Thousands of years ago, the ancient Egyptians left behind intricate inscriptions and depictions that offer insight into their beliefs about the afterlife. They envisioned a journey of being lifted up high or sent to the fire, highlighting their profound understanding of existence beyond earthly life. The Egyptians held a firm conviction in an afterlife, much like how they believed that cats could see demons, demonstrating the depth of their spiritual convictions.

In the civilizations of ancient Greece and Rome, belief in an afterlife also prevailed. These cultures worshiped multiple gods but shared a common understanding of life beyond the mortal realm. The concept of a heavenly existence was prominent, echoing the idea that there was more to life than what could be experienced on Earth. Beliefs played a significant role in shaping their spiritual and philosophical perspectives.

In biblical times, the people of Asia Minor held various beliefs about the afterlife, with many envisioning a heavenly existence governed by multiple gods and goddesses. Ancient civilizations embraced diverse religious practices, and mythologies centered around the concept of an afterlife.

Similarly, the Aztec Indians, from 1300 to 1500 AD, also held rich beliefs in an afterlife and revered multiple gods and goddesses in their spiritual traditions. Many of these spiritual beliefs were intertwined with the reverence for the divine concept of Mother Earth, emphasizing a deep connection to the natural world and the cosmos. These beliefs shaped their understanding of the afterlife and influenced their cultural and religious practices. Their society was deeply rooted in rituals of human sacrifice to appease their gods.

In India and Indonesia, we see Hinduism, and prayers are offered to a variety of gods and goddesses. Each deity represents different aspects of the divine and may be invoked for specific purposes such as wisdom, prosperity, or protection. In Buddhism, prayers are focused on attaining enlightenment and liberation from suffering. Buddhists may recite mantras, chants, and prayers to the historical Buddha. Yoga has its roots in ancient India and is an integral part of Hinduism and Buddhism. While some Christians may have concerns about the self-realization and inner divinity aspects of yoga, many people practice it for its physical and mental health benefits rather than its spiritual components. The beliefs of islanders were a combination of spiritual beliefs in multiple gods and a deep reverence for nature. Their spirituality was intertwined with the natural world.

In this vast human belief system, we can observe a multitude of perspectives on the afterlife, spiritual practices, and the concept of divinity. It's fascinating to see how different civilizations developed unique mythologies, religious rituals, and philosophical ideologies to make sense of existence beyond the earthly realm. Throughout history, these varied beliefs have shaped cultures, traditions, and societal norms in profound ways. Today, with the diversity of beliefs and non-beliefs in different parts of the world, the mission to spread the message of Jesus and the Gospel continues to be a driving force for many, reflecting the enduring significance of spiritual teachings and the pursuit of understanding the human experience.

## Powerful Moments

A woman who had been suffering from a hemorrhage for twelve years believed that she would be healed if she could just touch the fringe of Jesus' cloak. When she did, Jesus realized that power had gone out from Him. He turned around in the crowd and asked, "Who touched my clothes?" Jesus recognized her faith and told her, "Take heart, daughter, your faith has healed you." And the woman was healed at that moment.

In Luke 5:12-16, Jesus encountered a leper who approached Him, seeking to be cleansed. Despite the social stigma and fear surrounding leprosy during that time, Jesus responded with deep empathy and healed the leper, touching him and saying, "Be clean." This compassionate act exemplifies Jesus' love and concern for those who were considered outcasts in society.

In Mark 10:46-52, Jesus and His disciples, together with a large crowd, were getting ready to leave the city. Jesus was traveling to Jerusalem, where He would be sacrificed. A blind man named Bartimaeus was sitting by the roadside begging. When he heard that it was Jesus of Nazareth, he began to shout, "Jesus, Son of David, have mercy on me!" Numerous people scolded him and told him to be quiet, but he shouted all the more, "Son of David, have mercy on me!" Jesus stopped and said, "Call him." So they called to the blind man, "Take heart! On your feet! He's calling you." Throwing his cloak aside, he jumped to his feet and came to Jesus. "What do you want me to do for you?" Jesus asked him. The blind man said, "Rabbi, I want to see." "Go," said Jesus, "your faith has healed you." Immediately, he received his sight and followed Jesus along the road.

When Jesus was on the cross, He stopped dying in order to hear a thief say, "Jesus, remember me when you come into your kingdom." Jesus answered him, "Truly I tell you, today you will be with me in paradise."

Jesus knows us better than we know ourselves.

Psalms 139:1-6 "O LORD, you have examined me and know all about me. You know when I sit down and when I get up. You know my thoughts before I think them."

Matthew 9:4 But Jesus, knowing their thoughts, said, "Why do you think evil in your hearts?"

Luke 12:2 "Nothing is covered up that will not be revealed, or hidden that will not be known."

Matthew 12:25 Knowing their thoughts, he said to them, "Every kingdom divided against itself is laid waste, and no city or house divided against itself will stand."

## Ghosts or Evil Spirits

Ghosts and evil spirits are often considered malevolent supernatural entities known as demons. The concept of ghosts is frequently linked to the notion of lingering spirits of the deceased in the earthly realm. However, the Bible teaches that the spirits of the deceased return to God, not remaining on Earth. Evil spirits, on the other hand, are viewed as entities that seek to inflict harm or exert influence in our realm. Here are some examples from Scripture:

Matthew 8:16 - "When evening came, many who were demon-possessed were brought to him, and he drove out the spirits with a word and healed all the sick."

Mark 5:8-13 - For Jesus had said to him, "Come out of this man, you impure spirit!" Then Jesus asked him, "What is your name?" "My name is Legion," he replied, "for we are many." And he begged Jesus again and again not to send them out of the area. A large herd of pigs was feeding on the nearby hillside. The demons begged Jesus, "Send us among the pigs; allow us to go into them." He gave them permission, and the impure spirits came out and went into the pigs. The herd, about two thousand in number, rushed down the steep bank into the lake and were drowned.

James 2:19 - "You believe that there is one God. Good! Even the demons believe that—and shudder."

Acts 19:12-13 - "So that even handkerchiefs and aprons that had touched him were taken to the sick, and their illnesses were cured, and the evil spirits left them."

Leviticus 19:31 - "Do not turn to mediums or seek out spiritists, for you will be defiled by them. I am the Lord your God."

Deuteronomy 18:10-12 - "Let no one be found among you who sacrifices their son or daughter in the fire, who practices divination or sorcery, interprets omens, engages in witchcraft, or casts spells, or who is a medium or spiritist or who consults the dead. Anyone who does these things is detestable to the Lord."

Ecclesiastes 9:5 - "For the living know that they will die, but the dead know nothing; they have no further reward, and even their name is forgotten."

Ecclesiastes 12:7 - "And the dust returns to the earth as it was, and the spirit returns to God who gave it."

Matthew 14:25-27 - "Shortly before dawn Jesus went out to them, walking on the lake. When the disciples saw him walking on the lake, they were terrified. 'It's a ghost,' they said, and cried out in fear. But Jesus immediately said to them: 'Take courage! It is I. Don't be afraid.'"

Throughout history, people have reported encountering unexplained phenomena that defy comprehension. Tales of hauntings, strange occurrences in houses and graveyards, eerie incidents in neighborhoods, and even unsettling experiences during routine activities like bus rides have been repeated by individuals from diverse cultural backgrounds. These stories are not limited to a specific region or era, as similar accounts of inexplicable events can be found across different countries and throughout history. The disciples themselves, while on a boat, mistook a figure for a ghost, demonstrating that such encounters were known in their time. This collective witness to the unexplained serves as a reminder that we are not alone on this planet, and the universal presence of such stories reflects a shared sense of mystery and awe in the face of the unknown. The widespread nature of these accounts underscores the palpable reality of these experiences, emphasizing that they are not fabrications or figments of imagination.

Amidst such tales of uncertainty and fear, the message of Jesus' teachings provides reassurance. His arrival was a means to offer salvation and protection, ensuring that none of us need to live in fear of harm. The universal nature of these encounters serves as a reminder that such phenomena are part of the human experience, and the teachings of Jesus provide comfort and guidance in the face of these occurrences.

# Rational Minds

Just as there is a wide range of education and intelligence among people, there is also a wide range of beliefs in the world. From uneducated individuals to highly educated professionals, anyone can be a believer or not. Recognize that intelligence and education don't solely determine anyone's beliefs. Each individual's belief system is influenced by factors such as personal experiences, upbringing, culture, and more.

In the same way, we should understand that people from various walks of life may interpret Bible verses differently. It's not just about intellectual capacity but also personal perspectives and beliefs. Whether a person is a doctor, philosopher, scientist, lawyer, engineer, professor, researcher, mathematician, economist, psychologist, astronomer, statistician, architect, linguist, computer scientist, or holds any other occupation, their beliefs are shaped by numerous factors beyond their professional expertise.

Consider the hypothetical example of 100 philosophers. Among them, 75 may not believe in Jesus, 15 might be undecided, and ten may have studied and put their trust in God's hands. This example reflects the unique nature of beliefs across professions and backgrounds. It's not limited to anyone specifically but encompasses all walks of life.

## Understanding Varied Mentalities

Nobody knows when the end times will be, although signs definitely indicate it's coming. It's biblically recorded that Satan and many others manipulate people through various means. There's a spread of deception, which distorts the truth and leads people astray from God. This could involve influencing individuals to prioritize sinful desires over spiritual growth, promoting division and conflict among societies, and elevating moral decay. Additionally, fallen angels use temptation, fear, and doubt to draw individuals away from their faith and toward darkness.

Biblical verses that remind us are:

1 Peter 5:8: "Be alert and of sober mind. Your enemy the devil prowls around like a roaring lion looking for someone to devour."

2 Corinthians 10:3-4: "For though we walk in the flesh, we do not war according to the flesh. For the weapons of our warfare are not carnal but mighty in God for pulling down strongholds."

James 4:7: "Submit yourselves, then, to God. Resist the devil, and he will flee from you."

Revelation 12:9: "The great dragon was hurled down, that ancient serpent called the devil, and Satan, who leads the whole world astray. He was hurled to the earth, and his angels with him."

2 Corinthians 11:14: "And no wonder, for Satan himself masquerades as an angel of light."

Revelation 9:14: "saying to the sixth angel which had the trumpet, Release the four angels which are bound in the great river Euphrates."

Matthew 4:10: Jesus said to him, "Away from me, Satan! For it is written, You shall worship the Lord your God, and him only shall you serve."

Challenges in the Academic World

Teachers face challenges when discussing God in the academic world for various reasons. The concept of God is deeply rooted in religious beliefs, and educational environments often strive to maintain neutrality and inclusivity. This poses challenges for teachers wishing to incorporate discussions about God, as they must balance comprehensive education with respect for diverse beliefs. The separation of church and state further complicates this, with legal and institutional constraints limiting the discussion of religious topics.

Furthermore, the diverse and multicultural nature of modern classrooms means that teachers must be mindful of presenting information about God in a way that is respectful and sensitive to students from various religious and non-religious backgrounds. It necessitates a thoughtful and nuanced approach to teaching about God, taking into account the diverse perspectives and beliefs held by students and their families.

# Concepts of Binary and Non-binary Spiritual Beliefs

Some individuals choose to pray to a non-binary God whose pronouns are plural. They represent their personal beliefs and interpretations of spirituality, expressing their understanding of the divine in a manner that aligns with their views on gender and identity. Concepts can vary widely among different belief systems and interpretations of non-spiritual teachings.

The theology of America often centers on individual happiness. An Almighty God will not approve of religious alterations based on a culture focused against Him. Jesus said He is the "I Am." The universe knows who God is. Jesus has the authority of Heaven and Earth. People can say whatever they want, as it's their life and choice, but the facts remain that you were born either XX chromosome female, XY chromosome male, or XXY chromosome for intersex. And Jesus will always be a He. No matter how you process the world around you, God loves you, and you will be held responsible for your actions.

## Diversity of Opinion Amongst Academics and Professionals

As students enter college or university, they may encounter professors and professionals with varying beliefs, including those who believe in Jesus and those who don't. Students need to understand that, regardless of the beliefs of their educators and peers, each person should put on the full armor of God. While this armor is primarily to protect against evil, it's also vital for everything that comes our way, including challenges from instructors, teachers, and professors.

In diverse academic and professional environments, students may interact with individuals who hold contrasting religious or spiritual beliefs. Some professors and professionals may openly profess their faith in Jesus, while others may adhere to different belief systems or none at all. Students need to recognize that diversity of opinion is inherent in academic and professional settings, and they should approach interactions with respect and an open mind while remaining steadfast in their faith.

Putting on the armor, as described in the Bible, empowers believers to stand firm in their beliefs and values while engaging with diverse perspectives. The belt of truth serves as a foundation for discerning knowledge and understanding differing viewpoints. The breastplate of righteousness protects the heart and character, guiding all to uphold moral integrity even amidst opposing opinions. The shoes of the gospel of peace enable students to approach discussions and debates with a spirit of peace and understanding, fostering constructive dialogue regardless of contrasting beliefs. The shield of faith provides a safeguard against doubts and challenges to one's beliefs, allowing students to uphold their faith amidst intellectual and philosophical debates. The helmet of salvation guards the mind and thoughts, ensuring that students remain rooted in their faith even when faced with skepticism or opposition. Finally, the sword of the Spirit, which is the word of God, equips students with the wisdom and discernment to engage in meaningful conversations about their faith and to address misconceptions or objections with clarity and conviction.

While pursuing higher education, students may encounter scholars and professionals with extensive knowledge and expertise. Academic accomplishments do not diminish the significance of their faith. Putting on the armor equips everyone to navigate intellectual challenges, potential skepticism, and varying opinions in a manner that upholds their beliefs and values while fostering mutual respect and understanding.

By embracing the diversity of opinion amongst academics and professionals, students can cultivate a resilient faith and a deepened understanding of their own beliefs. Ultimately, through the application of the spiritual armor described in the Book of Ephesians, everybody can remain steadfast in their faith and values.

# The 4 D's of Faith

Matthew 14:29-30: He said, "Come." Then Peter got out of the boat, walked on the water, and came toward Jesus. But when he saw the wind, he was afraid, and beginning to sink, cried out, "Lord, save me!"

We need to believe in Christ with all our hearts. As you can see, with confidence, we can accomplish anything; Peter walked on water! But what happened? He took his eyes off Jesus, became afraid, and started sinking. In that moment of divine connection, Peter defied the laws of nature and stepped out in faith onto the water. With his eyes locked on Jesus, his faith propelled him forward, guiding each step with a sense of purpose and determination. However, as the winds howled and the waves crashed around him, Peter's faith wavered. He allowed fear to creep into his heart, causing him to doubt the very source of his strength. Yet, even in his moment of weakness, Jesus was there to extend a saving hand. With unwavering love and compassion, he reached out to Peter, lifting him from the depths of uncertainty and restoring him above the waves. It was a powerful reminder that even when we falter or lose sight, Jesus is always there to lift us up and guide us back to safety. When our faith is persistent, we tap into a reservoir of courage that empowers us to achieve remarkable accomplishments. It's a timeless lesson of keeping our eyes firmly fixed on Jesus. When we believe in him with all our hearts, there's nothing we cannot accomplish. With confidence, we can weather any storm, overcome any obstacle, and walk boldly into the future that he has planned for us.

Matthew 28:18: "Then Jesus came to them and said, All authority in heaven and on earth has been given to me."

It doesn't matter what spiritual warfare is going on; nothing is outside the power of God! This Earth is His footstool. When the day comes and we pass away, nobody else will be in that casket with you. There's no taking your trophies, collectibles, money, best friends, or worst enemies down with you.

Matthew 10:28: "Do not be afraid of those who kill the body but cannot kill the soul. Rather, be afraid of the One who can destroy both soul and body in hell."

## Deciding

We cannot outsmart God; only He can wash the evil away from our hearts. In Mark 7:8, Jesus rebukes the Pharisees, saying, "You have let go of the commands of God and are holding on to human traditions." Jesus didn't preach or teach a religion or a denomination. Be cautious of all the human additions and supplementary opinions. If we don't know what the Bible states and everything that Jesus taught, it's pretty easy to get derailed. You have to know what's right and wrong, and you cannot rely on others.

It's your walk and relationship with Christ.

Ezekiel 36:27 states, "And I will put my Spirit in you and move you to follow my decrees and be careful to keep my laws." The Holy Spirit empowers believers to follow God's commandments. It emphasizes that God's will should be carried out rather than our own.

If you, or anyone else, needs to be saved, deciding to follow Jesus can begin with a prayer like this:

I believe with all my heart that Jesus died for my sins and was resurrected on the third day. I repent of my wrongdoings and ask for forgiveness. I accept Jesus as my Lord and my Savior.

Trusting in your spiritual calling is more than a step; it's a leap for many. But once you're ready to fully commit and embrace your faith, even without directly witnessing Jesus, you'll understand the reasons behind His departure and the entrance of the Holy Spirit. The choice to follow Jesus is challenging but needs to be made nonetheless. As Jesus said, go and make disciples; it's evident that Jesus doesn't want you keeping your faith to yourself. The importance of sharing with others is equal to defending your beliefs.

When we choose to follow Jesus, we unlock the door, discovering the role that God intends for us. When we entrust our lives, we exhibit bravery, even amidst moments that may seem intimidating. You're the only one who can acknowledge Jesus as your Lord and Savior. No one else can save you, and you cannot save another person after they have passed away.

Each individual has only one lifetime to determine the course of their eternity.

God understands your aspirations and will guide you in the right direction. Upholding your faith marks the beginning of a challenging yet ultimately fulfilling journey. It's your decision to trust in God and follow the path He's laid out for you or turn your back against Him. Each of us paves our destiny with how we utilize our time. Giving your time and energy to God is one of the greatest investments because it'll pay dividends.

The Holy Spirit can give you peace, wisdom, and joy. Since time is a precious currency, wouldn't you want all the blessings you could have? Thousands of people are upset with God because they believe everything from prayers to solutions should be answered promptly. God doesn't live in our time. He lives in eternity as the Alpha and the Omega, the beginning and the end. God doesn't live by our deadlines.

Faith is not simply wishful thinking. It's a conscious decision to trust in something beyond ourselves and to seek a deeper understanding of God's objectives. Faith requires openness, humility, and a willingness to embark on a journey of exploration and growth. Each step taken in faith results in increased knowledge and spiritual development. In this adventure of life, having questions and concerns is normal.

Don't let anything discourage you; instead, use it as an opportunity to delve deeper into God's purpose.

You need to develop yourself, knowing what's biblical and what's made up. There's a lot of information out there, just like what the Pharisees were teaching and preaching from the fifth century BC to the first century AD. When they encountered Jesus, they clashed at every turn, unlike us, who may not challenge the status quo. Jesus rebuked their teachings and ensured everything was recorded for future generations to read, comprehend, and utilize the facts.

Throughout the Bible, many leaders wanted to control the scriptures and have power over the people. The same thing happens today. Jesus was humble and meek, washed feet, and mingled with the sinners and those who were poor and weak. Be cautious of all those who splendor in their buildings, individuals with gold and jewelry, and people kissing their hands and bowing down to them. Only God is called Father; nobody other than your earthly father should have that title.

The fact that the people and the leaders of the synagogues chased Jesus out and tried to kill him was a clear indication that they refused to believe who He was. At the same time, it was the Romans who crucified Jesus on the Cross. It was apparent that everyone was out to get Him, and He already knew it was coming. Rome ended up getting conquered around 455 AD, but in the early 300s, they began working hard and fast to take over the church as a source of power and authority. Like a few religions, some denominations are more sophisticated and secretive than the United States FBI.

It's your role to know whether you follow Jesus or yourself. We must understand that Jesus and the Heavenly Kingdom are free for the taking. There are no secrets. You must grow, educate yourself, and get involved!

## Developing

The Christian faith can be divided into four primary stages: exploration, commitment, maturing, and service. It doesn't matter if you feel like you have all the answers. Each of us needs to increase our prayers and strengthen our relationship with God. We must make an effort to study God's Word and reflect on what Jesus has taught; people aren't bothering to pick up a Bible. Too many religions are teaching against the Word of God. Becoming a disciple of Jesus Christ involves publicly acknowledging Jesus Christ as Lord and Savior and committing to model one's life after what He's done for you.

The exploration of your faith should drive you to think for yourself and prove or disprove what is currently being taught or stated versus what the Word of God says. Jesus exemplified obedience to God's commands, a prayer life, and the gospel proclamation. There are four critical factors to ensure you understand the big picture. Some of these have been intentionally restated because repetition is necessary on these topics, as so many people keep overlooking what's happening around them.

Breaking Scripture: Any religion telling you that you can pray to angels, any deceased humans, prophets alive or dead, or the earthly mother of Jesus, Mary, is against the word of God.

1 Timothy 2:5: "For there is one God and one mediator between God and mankind, the man Christ Jesus."

Revelation 22:8-9: "I, John, am the one who heard and saw these things. And when I had heard and seen them, I fell down to worship at the feet of the angel who had been showing them to me. But he said to me, 'Don't do that! I am a fellow servant with you and with your fellow prophets and with all who keep the words of this scroll. Worship God!'"

Idolizing: When any faith holding in consensus worships or prays to anything or anyone is guilty of idolatry. You cannot pray to dead humans, statues, paintings, or works of gold and silver. The Apostles were individuals doing the will of God, just like many who are doing God's work right now.

Exodus 20:4-6: "You shall not make for yourself an image in the form of anything in heaven above or on the earth beneath or in the waters below. You shall not bow down to them or worship them; for I, the Lord your God, am a jealous God, punishing the children for the sin of the parents to the third and fourth generation of those who hate me, but showing love to a thousand generations of those who love me and keep my commandments."

1 John 5:21: "Dear children, keep yourselves from idols."

Spiritual warfare is a scary subject for many, as it should be. Many people have seen the shadows that walk among us, slightly darker than the night. Others feel the presence of something nearby. What we see, feel, and experience are demons known as shadows. They are very real; their eyes can glow. They enjoy shadowing individuals and creating feelings of unease, among other behaviors that I'd rather not explain at this time for your peace of mind.

If you haven't been exposed to it, please don't go looking for it. The mind is delicate, and some people believe they can "handle it," but there are certain things in life that, once seen or learned, cannot be unseen or unlearned.

If you have no idea about spiritual warfare or what I'm covering, feel blessed, but understand that it happens with or without your knowledge. We are not alone on this planet. Don't think for a second you could outwit an angel; assume they'd know the Bible better than you do. Satan was quoting scripture to Jesus. For the record, if you're experiencing spiritual combat, you must urgently pray and ask for God's help. He has the power to remove the shadows from your presence or alter your sight, unable to see what's flowing through the realms.

In the Book of Acts, the Apostles confronted and expelled demons from possessed individuals. Such acts required not only unwavering faith but also a deep connection with God, a task only undertaken by those profoundly devoted to their faith and in close communion with the divine. Many believe they have what it takes to cleanse someone's spirit or defeat the fallen. The human mind and body are weak if you're not walking with the Lord, and even the best of the best can be subjected to devastation.

Ephesians 6:12: "For our struggle is not against flesh and blood, but against the rulers, against the authorities, against the powers of this dark world and against the spiritual forces of evil in the heavenly realms."

Leviticus 20:6: "I will set my face against anyone who turns to mediums and spiritists to prostitute themselves by following them, and I will cut them off from their people."

1 Samuel 28:11-14: Then the woman asked, "Whom shall I bring up for you? Bring up Samuel," he said. When the woman saw Samuel, she cried out at the top of her voice and said to Saul, "Why have you deceived me? You are Saul." The king said to her, "Don't be afraid. What do you see?" The woman said, "I see a ghostly figure coming up out of the earth." What does he look like? he asked. "An old man wearing a robe is coming up," she said. "Then Saul knew it was Samuel, and he bowed down with his face to the ground."

Saul was fooled, wanting to see Samuel to get some answers in desperate times. It was actually a demonic spirit impersonating him. This is why it's important not to focus on the dead and keep your eyes on God.

Developing a strong motivation to enhance your spirituality is necessary. Without feeling that inner yearning, nothing else will matter. If you're determined, nothing can stand in your way. This motivation involves prioritizing spiritual activities like studying the Bible, praying, and attending worship services, even when you lack the desire to participate. Since people are lazy, maintaining faith can be challenging; building the necessary discipline is the best thing you can do.

Like a seed, our faith must be nourished to sprout and develop into a full-grown plant. It has to mature before it can start producing results. In 2 Corinthians 9:6: "Whoever sows sparingly will also reap sparingly, and whoever sows generously will also reap generously." It's not a goal that can be accomplished in a single day but rather a process that develops over time.

Pursuing the Word of God and reflecting on His holy composure in our lives are two of the most important things we can do. Growth requires consistent reading of the Bible, in-depth study of its teachings, and the incorporation of those instructions into our daily lives. It's paramount for our development that we set aside time for prayer, both individually and as a community. When anyone gives their life to God, we are given our golden ticket into Heaven. The secret word was "Gives"; holding back yourself isn't the same thing.

## Deploying

We each carry a distinct purpose and calling bestowed by God's power. Taking the first step toward fulfilling this purpose requires putting our faith into practice. In terms of spiritual practice, what does it mean to 'walk the talk'? It's about actively living out our faith and demonstrating our obedience to the divine will by aligning our actions with our beliefs.

The Bible abounds with tales of people who exhibited steadfast faith in the face of daunting trials, only to witness miraculous responses from God to their prayers. Abraham serves as a prime example of this principle. When God directed him to relocate his family to an unfamiliar place, far from his known surroundings, Abraham faced uncertainty regarding his destination and future. Despite these uncertainties, he willingly obeyed God's command, putting his faith to the test. Consequently, God showered blessings upon him in ways he could never have anticipated or prepared for.

If you're feeling lost and uncertain about your purpose, take a step of faith. Follow the path directed by God and witness His reaction. You may be surprised by how He uses you to bless others and advance His kingdom. Taking action is crucial for spiritual growth. Central to your faith is the belief in God's existence and His individual plan for each person, along with the responsibility to live in accordance with that plan.

Discovering and following God's plan should be the primary focus. It entails being receptive to His guidance and obedient to His will, even if it contradicts our understanding. This involves being open to God's direction and making the willful choice to carry out His will, even when it's difficult or unpopular. It means adhering to God's commands, even if they go against prevailing societal norms. Furthermore, it entails not only adhering to one's convictions when convenient but consistently and unwaveringly. Essentially, it's about choosing to follow Christ regardless of the consequences. It requires the discipline to resist worldly temptations that lead away from God and toward self-centeredness. Transforming one's thoughts and actions to better reflect Christ's love to those around is essential for becoming more Christ-like.

Deploying one's faith means making it actionable. Mere belief is insufficient; faith must be put into practice. This involves trusting in God and sharing one's beliefs with others. When we trust in God and His abilities, we position ourselves for success. By making this declaration, we commit to doing whatever is necessary to fulfill His plans. We openly acknowledge our trust in His ability to work through us. Through obedience, we create an environment conducive to miraculous occurrences, increasing our likelihood of encountering them. I've been a part of many miracles, and all of us who've experienced them will never forget.

# Delivering

The message to a non-believer can come with significant costs. You may feel you've wasted your time, or perhaps you've planted a seed and done your part, hoping it will grow within them over time. Other times, you hit the mark, and the individual understands where you're coming from and the importance of making life changes. Sharing your faith is like public speaking; it's similar to stand-up comedy. You can get booed or hear applause. Either way, making disciples is a direct order regardless of how anyone takes the message.

The message was delivered to those closest to Jesus, and each of them made decisions nobody thought possible. Over the years, people have questioned whether Judas Iscariot would end up in hell after following Jesus and then betraying Him for 30 pieces of silver. The answer is no, just like Peter, who denied knowing Jesus three times in public. The prophet David wrote in Psalms 41:9, "Even my close friend in whom I trusted, who ate my bread, has lifted his heel against me."

In Luke 22:34, Jesus says, "I tell you, Peter, before the rooster crows today, you will deny three times that you know me." These circumstances were prophesied; Jesus knew the moment Satan would enter Judas' body and the aftermath. After Satan left Judas' body, he felt guilty about betraying an innocent man. He spoke to the high priests, who shrugged him off, and Judas threw the money back into the temple. The emotional pain was too difficult to handle, and Judas hanged himself. Though it seems outlandish, everything happened for God's purposes.

During the crucifixion, all the Apostles fled, which turned out to be a good thing; otherwise, they might have been killed, and the gospel would have been stopped. These men were overwhelmed by guilt and despair, trying to process everything that happened and burying the situations deep down inside. Everyone struggles to handle the truth and becomes defensive about it. Each person faces reality differently. John 10:10 says, "The thief comes only to steal and kill and destroy; I have come that they may have life, and have it to the full."

Many people out there have ears wide open, observing and absorbing all sorts of worldly corruption. The Bible states that one-third of the fallen angels are among us. From as far back as history records, many of them work to disrupt humanity and intentionally lead people astray. God has control over this world, but that doesn't mean you won't be tempted.

As we deliver the message to those willing to listen, we must guard our hearts and minds and encourage others to do the same. If people continue sinful activities, the door remains open for manipulation. None of us want the evil of the world to infiltrate our lives. People usually have good intentions; they don't want to be depressed or anxious. However, when we are careless due to negligence, we may not recognize attacks on our lives until it's too late.

As we teach and educate, we must be aware of what's happening in our lives and homes. There's spiritual warfare out there; discern between good and evil. Study God's Word; understand what is from God and what is from man.

The world isn't fair; be on guard. Watch what you see and hear, as the mind can start to enjoy negative influences and take you on a destructive journey.

## Final Thoughts

Thank you for taking charge of your life and seeking more. God chose you, and that journey brings many battles. Overcoming obstacles is necessary to receive more from Him. You're entrusted to do what's right in the eyes of the Lord. Jesus calls you to be faithful and prepared for evil. Though we live in this world, we're meant for a better place in eternity.

Renew your mind and be transformed.

Remember, God is not a delivery service. Don't pray only for your wants and needs; ask God what He desires for you. The answers might not always align with your wishes, but true blessings come from Him, not from earthly gains. God doesn't aim to make life difficult, but you will face challenges.

Judgment Day is a reality for us all. Our eternal fate will be decided, and that decision will be final. When you stand before God, it will just be you and Him. What will you say? Those not listed in the Book of Life will be cast into the lake of fire.

Ecclesiastes 12:14: "For God will bring every deed into judgment, including every hidden thing, whether it is good or evil."

Revelation 21:8: "But the cowardly, unbelieving, abominable, murderers, sexually immoral, sorcerers, idolaters, and all liars shall have their part in the lake which burns with fire and brimstone, which is the second death."

Be strong and courageous as you pursue your relationship with the Lord. Allow the Spirit to guide you and trust Him, even when the path seems unclear. Remember, not every detour is part of God's plan. Wear the full armor of God to discern your path. Commit to your faith without being swayed by worldly temptations, for whoever is a friend of the world is an enemy of God.

Please leave a review and check out more of my work at:

www.GarySPark.com

God Bless!

Milton Keynes UK
Ingram Content Group UK Ltd.
UKHW021633011224
451755UK00010B/608